Comprehension
Teacher's Guide 1

John Jackman

William Collins' dream of knowledge for all began with the publication of his first book in 1819. A self-educated mill worker, he not only enriched millions of lives, but also founded a flourishing publishing house. Today, staying true to this spirit, Collins books are packed with inspiration, innovation and practical expertise. They place you at the centre of a world of possibility and give you exactly what you need to explore it.

Collins. Freedom to teach.

Published by Collins
An imprint of HarperCollins*Publishers* Ltd.
77–85 Fulham Palace Road
Hammersmith
London
W6 8JB

**Browse the complete Collins catalogue at
www.collinseducation.com**

Text © John Jackman 2011
Design and illustrations © HarperCollins*Publishers* 2011

10 9 8 7 6 5 4 3 2 1

ISBN: 978-0-00-741066-8

John Jackman asserts his moral right to be identified as the author of this work.

British Library Cataloguing in Publication Data
A Catalogue record for this publication is available from the British Library.

Cover template: Laing & Carroll
Cover illustration: Steve Evans
Series design: Neil Adams and Garry Lambert
Picture research: Gill Metcalfe
Illustrations: Maggie Brand, Rob Englebright, Bethan Matthews, Andrew Midgley, Lisa Smith, Shirley Chiang, Bridget Dowty, Julian Mosedale, James Walmesley

Photographs
p54, top left: Lester Lefkowitz/Corbis; p54 top right: WoodyStock/Alamy; p54 bottom left: Rosenfield Images Ltd/Science Photo Library; p54 bottom right: David Marsden/Photolibrary

Printed and bound by Hobbs the Printers, UK.

Contents

Welcome to *Collins Primary Focus: Comprehension*

Comprehension is one of the keys to literacy. Most teachers of younger children will have encountered many who learn the decoding skills of reading only to stumble when questions are asked about the content of what has been read. Even when 'literal' interpretation of a text can be achieved there are many other, higher-order skills to be taught and learnt if the children are to gain fully from the process of reading – be it for pleasure or as the key tool in their academic growth and development.

This new edition of *Collins Primary Focus: Comprehension* contains a range of new material in the *Pupil Books*. This is supported by extensive notes and guidance now provided in separate *Teacher's Guides* at each level. Each unit of work contains passages to read and questions to answer that have been carefully chosen to excite, interest and motivate children to take their reading and study further.

Collins Primary Focus: Comprehension is designed to support your literacy teaching. The integrated *Pupil Book* and *Teacher's Guide* are based around a variety of comprehension passages and can be used to provide support, practice, consolidation and extension of the four core literacy skills: reading, writing, speaking and listening.

Each unit is linked by genre to *Collins Primary Literacy* (CPL) units at the appropriate level. The two series can be integrated to add depth to work undertaken on each genre of text.

Components of the programme

Age 6+

Introductory Pupil Book
978-0-00-741059-0

Introductory Teacher's Guide
978-0-00-741065-1

Age 7+

Pupil Book 1
978-0-00-741060-6

Teacher's Guide 1
978-0-00-741066-8

Age 8+

Pupil Book 2
978-0-00-741061-3

Teacher's Guide 2
978-0-00-741067-5

Age 9+

Pupil Book 3
978-0-00-741062-0

Teacher's Guide 3
978-0-00-741068-2

Age 10+

Pupil Book 4
978-0-00-741064-4

Teacher's Guide 4
978-0-00-741069-9

Teaching comprehension: the theory

Collins Primary Focus: Comprehension provides a structured programme for the teaching of reading comprehension. It will equip children for:
- reading the lines
- reading between the lines
- reading beyond the lines.

Skill areas

Comprehension questioning can be developed from a structure of thinking skills that ranges from simple recall to evaluation and response:

1. Knowledge	Who? What? When? Where? How?
2. Comprehension	What is meant by …? Explain …
3. Application	What other examples are there?
4. Analysis	What is the evidence for …?
5. Synthesis	How could we add to, improve, design, solve …?
6. Evaluation	What do you think about …?

Source: *Bloom's Taxonomy*

Collins Primary Focus: Comprehension applies these six thinking skills to the five important comprehension skill areas:

1. Literal comprehension

2. Reorganisation

3. Inferential and deductive comprehension

4. Evaluation

5. Appreciation

Source: Thomas Barrett in *Reading Today and Tomorrow* (University of London Press)

The activities in *Collins Primary Focus: Comprehension* develop each of these five skill areas and relate them to appropriate reading tasks. Broadly speaking, the five skill areas increase in difficulty from literal comprehension to appreciation. There is a clear progression throughout the five books, enabling children to develop the complete range of comprehension skills as they work through the series.

1. Literal comprehension

Literal comprehension focuses on the facts and ideas contained in a reading passage. Appropriate questions in each unit allow children to practise the recognition of:
- information explicitly stated, such as detail of characters and settings
- the main ideas
- key sequences of events
- comparisons of characters, times and places
- cause and effect – the reasons why certain things happen.

You can arrange activities so that children can answer with the text open in front of them for reference, or with the book closed so that they must recall what is in the text. Such recall exercises, significantly more demanding, are an important part of the group of skills which make up effective reading comprehension.

2. Reorganisation

Reorganisation requires children to analyse, or generally organise, information which is explicit. Questions and tasks in each unit require children to:
- classify people, things, places, events
- outline, summarise and synthesise.

3. Inferential and deductive comprehension

Inferential comprehension entails using the ideas and information explicitly provided in the text, and applying logical processes to them.

Deductive comprehension tasks are similar but also require the application of intuition and personal experience to draw conclusions. By implication, the thinking and imagination required by deductive comprehension will go beyond information which is immediately available in the text. The tasks relate to:
- supporting detail which the author has not seen fit to provide
- inferring the main idea, when it is not explicitly provided
- sequencing, most frequently in terms of what might be expected to happen next or what will be the eventual outcome
- providing comparisons between characters, times and places
- relating cause and effect relationships; hypothesising about character motivations and intentions
- interpreting figurative language.

4. Evaluation

Evaluation implies the making of judgements about a reading passage with outside criteria, including children's own evolving personal values and moral code.

In the teaching context, it is important to encourage, among other things, the qualities of accuracy and logic, and the ability to assess desirability and probability. These can require the evaluation of:
- reality and fantasy (could this really have happened?)
- fact and opinion (what is the author's evidence? Is the reader being manipulated?)
- validity (how does the information match up to that from other sources?)
- desirability (was a character right to act in a given way?).

5. Appreciation

Appreciation combines all the other dimensions of reading comprehension, dealing as it does with the aesthetic and psychological impact of the text. It calls for children to interact with the passage through:

- emotional response to the content in terms of interest, excitement, amusement, fear and other such emotions
- sympathy for or empathy with characters or situations
- reactions to the author's use of language and imagery.

See p43 for a chart listing the question types used in this level of the programme.

Comprehension within literacy teaching

Collins Primary Focus: Comprehension builds the five comprehension skill areas into broader literacy activities. Each unit in the *Teacher's Guide* identifies learning objectives from the 12 Literacy Framework strands, to fully integrate the key skills of reading, writing, speaking and listening.

1. Speaking

2. Listening and responding

3. Group discussion and interaction

4. Drama

5. Word recognition: decoding (reading) and encoding (spelling)

6. Word structure and spelling

7. Understanding and interpreting texts

8. Engaging and responding to texts

9. Creating and shaping texts

10. Text structure and organization

11. Sentence structure and punctuation

12. Presentation

The learning objectives listed within each unit are preceded by a number which relates to one of the 12 strands above.

Using *Collins Primary Focus: Comprehension*

Collins Primary Focus: Comprehension is made up of units that have been devised in order to develop, from the beginning, the range of the five important comprehension skill areas. The level of skill that is required becomes increasingly sophisticated as the course progresses.

Each book contains carefully structured units, each of which include one or more passages of text. In addition, there are Progress Units designed to evaluate children's skill development and progress. The Introductory book contains 13 teaching units and one Progress Unit; all other books have 20 teaching units and two Progress Units. The units in all five books follow the same structure. Every unit of work is organised around three headings: *Do you remember?*, *More to think about* and *Now try these*.

The *Do you remember?* questions, which require a literal response to the text, are likely to be the least challenging. They have been written to be accessible to the majority of children. The *More to think about* questions are more difficult and the *Now try these* questions are more demanding still.

The course has been designed to be straightforward and easy to use. If you feel it is appropriate, you can use the material in the context of whole-class teaching. Equally, this material is flexible and can be used by individuals or small groups at their own pace.

In the context of whole-class teaching, it is suggested that the first part of each lesson should be to read aloud the passage of text. Follow this by discussing the stimulus material, including the illustrations, and tackle some selected questions together with the class. The questions allow for group work, and have been prepared to ensure a minimum of teacher intervention. This will enable you to then spend time with groups as they undertake different sections of the work.

The *Teacher's Guide* provides information about each unit so that you can set your comprehension lessons within the context of your overall literacy teaching. Learning objectives, cross-curricular links and assessment focuses are provided to assist with planning and assessment before and after you use each unit.

Each *Teacher's Guide* unit also includes more reading, writing, speaking and listening activities for you to use before and after the children have completed the *Pupil Book* work.

A *Pupil Book* unit

Unit number for clear navigation through the book.

Context box provides background information where necessary.

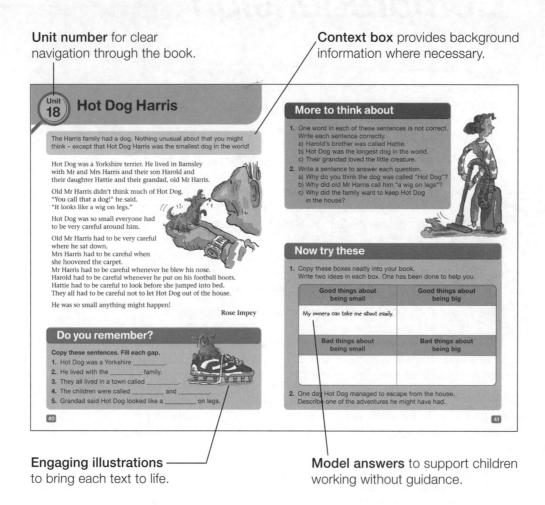

Engaging illustrations to bring each text to life.

Model answers to support children working without guidance.

Do you remember?

Reading the lines:

- literal comprehension (easier recognition and recall activities).

More to think about

Reading between the lines:

- literal comprehension (more challenging recognition and recall activities)
- reorganisation (classifying; summarising and synthesising)
- inferential and deductive comprehension (supporting detail; the main idea; sequencing; comparison of characters, settings; cause and effect; character traits; prediction).

Now try these

Reading beyond the lines:

- evaluation (reality/fantasy; fact/opinion; validity; appropriateness; acceptability)
- appreciation (emotional response; empathy with characters or incidents; understanding of, and reactions to, use of language and imagery).

A *Teacher's Guide* unit

Unit number for clear navigation through the book.

Genre of passage taken from the current Literacy Framework.

Learning objectives taken from the relevant year of the current Literacy Framework. The numbers refer to the 12 Framework strands (see p8). Reading objectives are listed first, with other objectives following.

Cross-curricular links taken from the National Curriculum Schemes of Work.

Each unit is matched to **Assessing Pupils' Progress**, with assessment focuses repeated next to each activity within the *Teacher's Guide* unit (see p13). AF = assessment focus; SL = speaking and listening; W = writing; R = reading.

Challenging **vocabulary** is identified for discussion before reading.

The **Collins Primary Literacy reference** links each unit to work on the same genre in CPL.

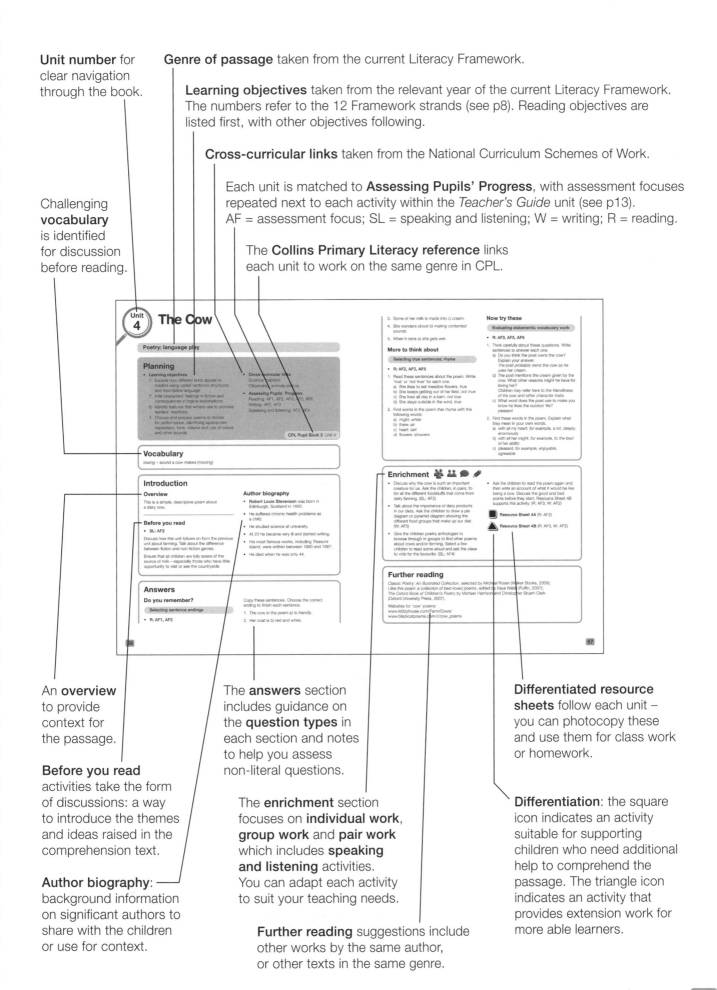

An **overview** to provide context for the passage.

Before you read activities take the form of discussions: a way to introduce the themes and ideas raised in the comprehension text.

Author biography: background information on significant authors to share with the children or use for context.

The **answers** section includes guidance on the **question types** in each section and notes to help you assess non-literal questions.

The **enrichment** section focuses on **individual work**, **group work** and **pair work** which includes **speaking and listening** activities. You can adapt each activity to suit your teaching needs.

Further reading suggestions include other works by the same author, or other texts in the same genre.

Differentiated resource sheets follow each unit – you can photocopy these and use them for class work or homework.

Differentiation: the square icon indicates an activity suitable for supporting children who need additional help to comprehend the passage. The triangle icon indicates an activity that provides extension work for more able learners.

Assessment

There are different ways of assessing progress in children's learning.

Formative assessment

Each unit in *Collins Primary Focus: Comprehension* provides opportunities for assessing reading, writing, speaking and listening skills, embedded in the every-day teaching and learning process.

Formative assessment or assessment for learning (AfL) is most effective when you:
- involve children in their own learning and share learning goals
- provide effective feedback to children
- adjust teaching as a result of assessment
- share with children how they can assess their own progress
- help children understand how to improve.

Summative assessment

Summative assessment is carried out periodically, for example at the end of a term, a year or a key stage. It is a judgement about children's performance at a certain point in time in relation to national standards.

Two Progress Units are provided within each *Pupil Book*, with the exception of the *Introductory Pupil Book* which has one. These units can be used for periodic assessment in a more formal setting.

Assessment Focuses (AFs)

Your judgements through formative and summative assessment can be combined to reach a conclusion about the level to which each child is working, following levelling guidelines.

Each activity in the programme is matched to the Assessment Focuses which make up the Assessing Pupils' Progress (APP) guidelines, indicating which activities can be used to collect evidence for each Assessment Focus. The Assessment Focuses are listed opposite for reference.

A class record sheet and an individual record sheet are provided within this section. These can be photocopied.

Reading Assessment Focuses (AFs)

AF1	Use a range of strategies, including accurate decoding of text, to read for meaning	
AF2	Understand, describe, select or retrieve information, events or ideas from texts and use quotation and reference to text	*literal and information retrieval*
AF3	Deduce, infer or interpret information, events or ideas from texts	*inference, deduction, prediction, using, where relevant, prior knowledge*
AF4	Identify and comment on the structure and organisation of texts, including grammatical and presentational features at text level	*organisation of content*
AF5	Explain and comment on writers' uses of language, including grammatical and literary features at word and sentence level	*reaction to use of language*
AF6	Identify and comment on writers' purposes and viewpoints and the overall effect of the text on the reader	*empathy and objective criticism*
AF7	Relate texts to their social, cultural and historical contexts and literary traditions	*contextual evaluation*

Writing Assessment Focuses (AFs)

AF1	Write imaginative, interesting and thoughtful texts
AF2	Produce texts which are appropriate to task, reader and purpose
AF3	Organise and present whole texts effectively, sequencing and structuring information, ideas and events
AF4	Construct paragraphs and use cohesion within and between paragraphs
AF5	Vary sentences for clarity, purpose and effect
AF6	Write with technical accuracy of syntax and punctuation in phrases, clauses and sentences
AF7	Select appropriate and effective vocabulary
AF8	Use correct spelling

Speaking and listening Assessment Focuses (AFs)

AF1	**Talking to others** Talk in purposeful and imaginative ways to explore ideas and feelings, adapting and varying structure and vocabulary according to purpose, listeners, and content
AF2	**Talking with others** Listen and respond to others, including in pairs and groups, shaping meanings through suggestions, comments, and questions
AF3	**Talking within role-play and drama** Create and sustain different roles and scenarios, adapting techniques in a range of dramatic activities to explore texts, ideas, and issues
AF4	**Talking about talk** Understand the range and uses of spoken language, commenting on meaning and impact and draw on this when talking to others

Class record sheet
Collins Primary Focus: Comprehension

It is suggested that you give a brief indication of children's progress for each unit:

/ = attempted; X = completed satisfactorily

Book _____

Class _____

Year _____

Names	Units																					
	1	2	3	4	5	6	7	8	9	10	A	11	12	13	14	15	16	17	18	19	20	B

Individual record sheet
Collins Primary Focus: Comprehension

Name _____

Book _____ Class _____ Year _____

Unit	Comment	Date
1		
2		
3		
4		
5		
6		
7		
8		
9		
10		
A		
11		
12		
13		
14		
15		
16		
17		
18		
19		
20		
B		

Unit by unit overview chart

Unit	Genre	PNS learning objectives	Cross-curricular links	Assessing Pupils' Progress
1 Monkey Business	*Non-fiction: reports* CPL Pupil Book 3 Unit 3	7: Identify and make notes of the main points of section(s) of text 8: Empathise with characters and debate moral dilemmas portrayed in texts 1: Sustain conversation, explain or give reasons for their views or choices 2: Follow up others' points and show whether they agree or disagree in whole-class discussion 9: Write non-narrative texts using structures of different text-types	Citizenship: in the media – what's the news? Science: plants and animals in the local environment	Reading: AF1, AF2, AF3, AF4 Writing: AF2, AF3, AF6 Speaking and listening: AF1, AF2
2 Caterpillars (Eric Slayter)	*Poetry: language play* CPL Pupil Book 3 Unit 4	7: Infer characters' feelings in fiction and consequences in logical explanations 7: Explore how different texts appeal to readers using varied sentence structures and descriptive language 8: Identify features that writers use to provoke readers' reactions 1: Choose and prepare poems or stories for performance, identifying appropriate expression, tone, volume and use of voices and other sounds 9: Write non-narrative texts using structures of different text-types 9: Select and use a range of technical and descriptive vocabulary	Science: plants and animals in the local environment; habitats; life cycles	Reading: AF1, AF2, AF3, AF5 Writing: AF1, AF6, AF7 Speaking and listening: AF2, AF4
3 Working on a Farm	*Non-fiction: information texts* CPL Pupil Book 3 Unit 11	7: Identify how different texts are organised, including reference texts, magazines and leaflets, on paper and on screen 1: Sustain conversation, explain or give reasons for their views or choices 2: Follow up others' points and show whether they agree or disagree in whole-class discussion 9: Write non-narrative texts using structures of different text-types 9: Use layout, format graphics and illustrations for different purposes	Geography: a contrasting locality; investigating our local area History: what was it like to live here in the past?	Reading: AF1, AF2, AF3 Writing: AF2, AF3, AF6 Speaking and listening: AF1, AF2

continued overleaf

#	Unit	Objectives	Cross-curricular links	Assessment focuses
4	**The Cow** (Robert Louis Stevenson) — *Poetry: language play* — **CPL Pupil Book 3** Unit 4	7: Explore how different texts appeal to readers using varied sentence structures and descriptive language 7: Infer characters' feelings in fiction and consequences in logical explanations 8: Identify features that writers use to provoke readers' reactions 1: Choose and prepare poems or stories for performance, identifying appropriate expression, tone, volume and use of voices and other sounds	Science: habitats Citizenship: animals and us	Reading: AF1, AF2, AF3, AF5, AF6 Writing: AF2, AF3 Speaking and listening: AF2, AF4
5	**Looking at Books** — *Non-fiction: information texts* — **CPL Pupil Book 3** Unit 11	7: Identify how different texts are organised, including reference texts, magazines and leaflets, on paper and on screen 8: Share and compare reasons for reading preferences, extending the range of books read 1: Sustain conversation, explain or give reasons for their views or choices in different contexts 1: Develop and use specific vocabulary in different contexts 2: Follow up others' points and show whether they agree or disagree in whole-class discussion 3: Actively include and respond to all members of the group 9: Select and use a range of technical and descriptive vocabulary	Design and technology: storybooks	Reading: AF1, AF2, AF3, AF4 Writing: AF2 Speaking and listening: AF1, AF2
6	**Gumdrop Has a Birthday** (Val Biro) — *Narrative: stories with familiar settings; significant authors* — **CPL Pupil Book 3** Unit 1	7: Infer characters' feelings in fiction and consequences in logical explanations 8: Empathise with characters and debate moral dilemmas portrayed in texts 1: Sustain conversation, explain or give reasons for their views or choices 2: Follow up others' points and show whether they agree or disagree in whole-class discussion 9: Write non-narrative texts using structures of different text-types	History: how has life in Britain changed since 1948?	Reading: AF1, AF2, AF3 Writing: AF2, AF3 Speaking and listening: AF1, AF2
7	**An Ants' Nest** — *Non-fiction: information texts* — **CPL Pupil Book 3** Unit 11	7: Identify and make notes of the main points of section(s) of text 7: Identify how different texts are organised, including reference texts, magazines and leaflets, on paper and on screen 1: Sustain conversation, explain or give reasons for their views or choices 2: Follow up others' points and show whether they agree or disagree in whole-class discussion 9: Write non-narrative texts using structures of different text-types	Science: habitats; plants and animals in the local environment; life cycles	Reading: AF1, AF2, AF3, AF4 Writing: AF1, AF6 Speaking and listening: AF2

Unit by unit overview chart *continued*

Unit	Genre	PNS learning objectives	Cross-curricular links	Assessing Pupils' Progress
8 **Thunder and Lightning**	*Narrative: myths and legends* **CPL Pupil Book 3** Unit 5	7: Infer characters' feelings in fiction and consequences in logical explanations 8: Empathise with characters and debate moral dilemmas portrayed in texts 1: Sustain conversation, explain or give reasons for their views or choices 2: Follow up others' points and show whether they agree or disagree in whole-class discussion 3: Actively include and respond to all members of the group 9: Use beginning, middle and end to write narratives in which events are sequenced logically and conflicts resolved	Geography: weather around the world	Reading: AF1, AF2, AF3, AF5, AF7 Writing: AF1, AF3, AF6 Speaking and listening: AF1, AF2, AF4
9 **The Lion and the Mouse** (Aesop)	*Narrative: myths and legends; significant authors* **CPL Pupil Book 3** Unit 5	7: Infer characters' feelings in fiction and consequences in logical explanations 8: Empathise with characters and debate moral dilemmas portrayed in texts 1: Sustain conversation, explain or give reasons for their views or choices 2: Follow up others' points and show whether they agree or disagree in whole-class discussion 3: Actively include and respond to all members of the group 9: Use beginning, middle and end to write narratives in which events are sequenced logically and conflicts resolved	Citizenship: choices	Reading: AF1, AF2, AF3 Writing: AF1, AF3, AF7 Speaking and listening: AF1, AF2
10 **The Dragon's Cold** (John Talbot)	*Narrative: stories with familiar settings* **CPL Pupil Book 3** Unit 1	7: Infer characters' feelings in fiction and consequences in logical explanations 8: Empathise with characters and debate moral dilemmas portrayed in texts 1: Sustain conversation, explain or give reasons for their views or choices 2: Follow up others' points and show whether they agree or disagree in whole-class discussion 9: Use beginning, middle and end to write narratives in which events are sequenced logically and conflicts resolved 9: Write non-narrative texts using structures of different text-types	Citizenship: animals and us	Reading: AF1, AF2, AF3 Writing: AF1, AF2, AF3, AF6 Speaking and listening: AF1, AF2, AF3
Progress Unit A Crash!	*Narrative: adventure and mystery* **CPL Pupil Book 3** Unit 10	7: Infer characters' feelings in fiction and consequences in logical explanations 8: Empathise with characters and debate moral dilemmas portrayed in texts 9: Use beginning, middle and end to write narratives in which events are sequenced logically and conflicts resolved 9: Use layout, format graphics and illustrations for different purposes	Citizenship: people who help us	Reading: AF1, AF2, AF3 Writing: AF3, AF6, AF7

continued overleaf

	Text	Objectives	Curriculum links	Assessment focuses
11 Fun on Bikes	*Non-fiction: information texts* **CPL Pupil Book 3** Unit 11	7: Identify how different texts are organised, including reference texts, magazines and leaflets, on paper and on screen 1: Sustain conversation, explain or give reasons for their views or choices 2: Follow up others' points and show whether they agree or disagree in whole-class discussion 3: Actively include and respond to all members of the group 9: Write non-narrative texts using structures of different text-types 9: Use layout, format graphics and illustrations for different purposes	PE: outdoor and adventurous activities	Reading: AF1, AF2, AF3, AF4, AF6 Writing: AF2, AF3, AF6 Speaking and listening: AF2
12 The Owl Who Was Afraid of the Dark (Jill Tomlinson)	*Narrative: stories with familiar settings; significant authors* **CPL Pupil Book 3** Unit 1	7: Infer characters' feelings in fiction and consequences in logical explanations 8: Empathise with characters and debate moral dilemmas portrayed in texts 1: Sustain conversation, explain or give reasons for their views or choices 2: Follow up others' points and show whether they agree or disagree in whole-class discussion 3: Actively include and respond to all members of the group 9: Use beginning, middle and end to write narratives in which events are sequenced logically and conflicts resolved	Science: plants and animals in the local environment; habitats Citizenship: living in a diverse world	Reading: AF1, AF2, AF3, AF5 Writing: AF1, AF7 Speaking and listening: AF1, AF2, AF4
13 Lost in the Zoo	*Non-fiction: instructions* **CPL Pupil Book 3** Unit 6	7: Identify how different texts are organised, including reference texts, magazines and leaflets, on paper and on screen 1: Sustain conversation, explain or give reasons for their views or choices 2: Follow up others' points and show whether they agree or disagree in whole-class discussion 9: Write non-narrative texts using structures of different text-types 9: Use layout, format graphics and illustrations for different purposes	Science: habitats Geography: geography and numbers	Reading: AF1, AF2, AF3, AF4 Writing: AF2, AF3, AF6 Speaking and listening: AF1, AF2
14 The Tale of Peter Rabbit (Beatrix Potter)	*Narrative: stories with familiar settings; significant authors* **CPL Pupil Book 3** Unit 1	7: Infer characters' feelings in fiction and consequences in logical explanations 8: Share and compare reasons for reading preferences, extending the range of books read 8: Empathise with characters and debate moral dilemmas portrayed in texts 1: Sustain conversation, explain or give reasons for their views or choices 2: Follow up others' points and show whether they agree or disagree in whole-class discussion 4: Present events and characters through dialogue to engage the interest of an audience 9: Use beginning, middle and end to write narratives in which events are sequenced logically and conflicts resolved	Science: plants and animals in the local environment	Reading: AF1, AF2, AF3 Writing: AF1, AF6 Speaking and listening: AF1, AF2, AF3

Unit by unit overview chart continued

Unit	Genre	PNS learning objectives	Cross-curricular links	Assessing Pupils' Progress
15 On Holiday	*Non-fiction: instructions* **CPL Pupil Book 3** Unit 6	7: Identify how different texts are organised, including reference texts, magazines and leaflets, on paper and on screen 1: Sustain conversation, explain or give reasons for their views or choices 2: Follow up others' points and show whether they agree or disagree in whole-class discussion 9: Write non-narrative texts using structures of different text-types	Geography: geography and numbers; going to the seaside Citizenship: how do rules and laws affect me?	Reading: AF1, AF2, AF3, AF4 Writing: AF2, AF6 Speaking and listening: AF1, AF2
16 Roger the Dog (Ted Hughes)	*Poetry: language play* **CPL Pupil Book 3** Unit 12	7: Infer characters' feelings in fiction and consequences in logical explanations 7: Explore how different texts appeal to readers using varied sentence structures and descriptive language 8: Share and compare reasons for reading preferences, extending the range of books read 1: Choose and prepare poems or stories for performance, identifying appropriate expression, tone, volume and use of voices and other sounds 3: Actively include and respond to all members of the group 9: Select and use a range of technical and descriptive vocabulary	Citizenship: animals and us	Reading: AF1, AF2, AF3, AF5 Writing: AF1, AF7 Speaking and listening: AF1, AF2, AF4
17 Gran's New House	*Narrative: letters* **CPL Pupil Book 3** Unit 9	7: Identify how different texts are organised, including reference texts, magazines and leaflets, on paper and on screen 1: Explain process or present information, ensuring that items are clearly sequenced, relevant details are included and accounts are ended effectively 9: Write non-narrative texts using structures of different text-types	Geography: a contrasting locality; going to the seaside	Reading: AF1, AF2, AF3, AF4 Writing: AF2, AF3, AF6 Speaking and listening: AF1, AF2
18 Hot Dog Harris (Rose Impey)	*Narrative: stories with familiar settings; significant authors* **CPL Pupil Book 3** Unit 1	7: Infer characters' feelings in fiction and consequences in logical explanations 8: Empathise with characters and debate moral dilemmas portrayed in texts 1: Sustain conversation, explain or give reasons for their views or choices 2: Follow up others' points and show whether they agree or disagree in whole-class discussion 9: Use beginning, middle and end to write narratives in which events are sequenced logically and conflicts resolved	Science: plants and animals in the local environment Citizenship: animals and us	Reading: AF1, AF2, AF3 Writing: AF1, AF6 Speaking and listening: AF2

		Objectives	Cross-curricular links	Assessment Focuses
19 Funny Feeders	*Non-fiction: information texts* CPL Pupil Book 3 Unit 11	7: Identify how different texts are organised, including reference texts, magazines and leaflets, on paper and on screen 7: Identify and make notes of the main points of section(s) of text 1: Sustain conversation, explain or give reasons for their views or choices 2: Follow up others' points and show whether they agree or disagree in whole-class discussion 9: Write non-narrative texts using structures of different text-types	Science: teeth and eating; variation	Reading: AF1, AF2, AF3, AF4 Writing: AF1, AF6 Speaking and listening: AF1, AF2
20 Mrs Wobble the Waitress (Allan and Janet Ahlberg)	*Narrative: stories with familiar settings; significant authors* CPL Pupil Book 3 Unit 1	7: Infer characters' feelings in fiction and consequences in logical explanations 7: Identify and make notes of the main points of section(s) of text 8: Empathise with characters and debate moral dilemmas portrayed in texts 1: Sustain conversation, explain or give reasons for their views or choices 2: Follow up others' points and show whether they agree or disagree in whole-class discussion 3: Actively include and respond to all members of the group 9: Use beginning, middle and end to write narratives in which events are sequenced logically and conflicts resolved 9: Write non-narrative texts using structures of different text-types	Citizenship: living in a diverse world	Reading: AF1, AF2, AF3 Writing: AF1, AF2, AF6 Speaking and listening: AF1, AF2
Progress Unit B **The Golly Sisters Go West** (Betsy Byars)	*Narrative: dialogue and plays; significant authors* CPL Pupil Book 3 Unit 2	7: Infer characters' feelings in fiction and consequences in logical explanations 7: Identify and make notes of the main points of section(s) of text 8: Empathise with characters and debate moral dilemmas portrayed in texts 9: Use beginning, middle and end to write narratives in which events are sequenced logically and conflicts resolved	Citizenship: animals and us Geography: where in the world is Barnaby Bear?	Reading: AF1, AF2, AF3 Writing: AF1, AF6

Curriculum for Excellence matching chart: Primary 4

Listening and Talking

	First Level	1	2	3	4	5	6	7	8	9	10	A	11	12	13	14	15	16	17	18	19	20	B
Enjoyment and choice	I regularly select and listen to or watch texts which I enjoy and find interesting, and I can explain why I prefer certain sources. I regularly select subject, purpose, format and resources to create texts of my choice. **LIT 1-01a**										✓					✓							
Tools for listening and talking	When I engage with others, I know when and how to listen, when to talk, how much to say, when to ask questions and how to respond with respect. **LIT 1-02a**	✓	✓	✓	✓	✓	✓	✓	✓	✓	✓		✓	✓	✓	✓	✓	✓	✓	✓	✓	✓	
	I am exploring how pace, gesture, expression, emphasis and choice of words are used to engage others and I can use what I learn. **ENG 1-03a**			✓						✓	✓					✓			✓				
Finding and using information	As I listen or watch, I can identify and discuss the purpose, key words and main ideas of the text, and use this information for a specific purpose. **LIT 1-04a**			✓				✓		✓										✓			
	As I listen or watch, I am learning to take notes under given headings and use these to understand what I have listened to or watched and create new texts. **LIT 1-05a**			✓				✓											✓	✓	✓		

continued overleaf

Category	Outcome																					
	I can select ideas and relevant information, organise these in a logical sequence and use words which will be interesting and/or useful for others. **LIT 1-06a**	✓				✓						✓				✓						
Understanding, analysing and evaluating	I can show my understanding of what I listen to or watch by responding to and asking different kinds of questions. **LIT 1-07a**	✓			✓				✓			✓				✓						
	To help me develop an informed view, I am learning to recognise the difference between fact and opinion. **LIT 1-08a**											✓										
Creating texts	When listening and talking with others, for different purposes, I can exchange information, experiences, explanations, ideas and opinions. **LIT 1-09a**	✓	✓	✓	✓	✓	✓	✓	✓	✓	✓	✓	✓	✓	✓	✓	✓	✓	✓	✓	✓	✓
	I can communicate clearly when engaging with others within and beyond my place of learning, using selected resources as required. **LIT 1-10a**	✓				✓						✓										

Curriculum for Excellence matching chart: Primary 4 *continued*

Reading	First Level	1	2	3	4	5	6	7	8	9	10	A	11	12	13	14	15	16	17	18	19	20	B
Enjoyment and choice	I regularly select and read, listen to or watch texts which I enjoy and find interesting, and I can explain why I prefer certain texts and authors. **LIT 1-11a**		✓		✓	✓												✓					
Tools for reading	I can use my knowledge of sight vocabulary, phonics, context clues, punctuation and grammar to read with understanding and expression. **ENG 1-12a**	✓		✓	✓	✓	✓	✓	✓	✓	✓	✓	✓	✓	✓	✓	✓	✓	✓	✓	✓	✓	✓
	I am learning to select and use strategies and resources, before I read and as I read, to help make the meaning of texts clear. **LIT 1-13a**	✓		✓		✓	✓	✓	✓	✓	✓	✓	✓	✓	✓	✓	✓	✓	✓	✓	✓	✓	✓
Finding and using information	Using what I know about the features of different types of texts, I can find, select, sort and use information for a specific purpose. **LIT 1-14a**					✓		✓									✓				✓		
	I am learning to make notes under the given headings and use these to understand information, explore ideas and problems and create new texts. **LIT 1-15a**	✓	✓	✓	✓	✓	✓	✓	✓	✓	✓	✓	✓	✓	✓	✓	✓	✓	✓	✓	✓	✓	✓

Understanding, analysing and evaluating	To show my understanding across different areas of learning, I can identify and consider the purpose and main ideas of my text. **LIT 1-16a**	To show my understanding, I can respond to different kinds of questions and other close reading tasks and I am learning to create some questions of my own. **ENG 1-17a**	To help me develop an informed view, I can recognise the difference between fact and opinion. **LIT 1-18a**	I can share my thoughts about structure, characters and/or setting, recognise the writer's message and relate it to my own experiences, and comment on the effective choice of words and other features. **ENG 1-19a**
(tick columns)	✓✓✓✓✓✓✓✓✓✓✓✓✓✓✓✓✓✓✓	✓✓✓✓✓✓✓✓✓✓✓✓✓✓✓✓✓✓✓	✓	✓✓✓✓✓✓✓✓✓✓✓✓✓✓✓✓✓✓✓

continued overleaf

Curriculum for Excellence matching chart: Primary 4 *continued*

Writing	First Level	1	2	3	4	5	6	7	8	9	10	A	11	12	13	14	15	16	17	18	19	20	B
Enjoyment and choice	I enjoy creating texts of my choice and I regularly select subject, purpose, format and resources to suit the needs of my audience. LIT 1-20a	✓	✓	✓			✓	✓				✓	✓		✓	✓	✓	✓	✓	✓	✓	✓	
Tools for writing	I can spell most commonly used words, use my knowledge of letter patterns and spelling rules and use resources to help me spell tricky or unfamiliar words. LIT 1-21a	✓	✓	✓	✓	✓	✓	✓	✓	✓	✓	✓	✓	✓	✓	✓	✓	✓	✓	✓	✓	✓	✓
	I can write independently, use appropriate punctuation and order my sentences in a way that makes sense. LIT 1-22a	✓	✓	✓	✓	✓	✓	✓	✓	✓	✓	✓	✓	✓	✓	✓	✓	✓	✓	✓	✓	✓	✓
	Throughout the writing process, I can check that my writing makes sense. LIT 1-23a	✓	✓	✓	✓	✓	✓	✓	✓	✓	✓	✓	✓	✓	✓	✓	✓	✓	✓	✓	✓	✓	✓
	I can present my writing in a way that will make it legible and attractive for my reader, combining words, images and other features. LIT 1-24a	✓					✓				✓	✓	✓		✓		✓	✓					

Organising and using information	I am learning to use my notes and other types of writing to help me understand information and ideas, explore problems, generate and develop ideas or create new text. **LIT 1-25a**
	By considering the type of text I am creating, I can select ideas and relevant information, organise these in a logical sequence and use words which will be interesting and/or useful for others. **LIT 1-26a**
Creating texts	I can convey information, describe events or processes, share my opinions or persuade my reader in different ways. **LIT 1-28a/LIT 1-29a**
	I can describe and share my experiences and how they made me feel. **ENG 1-30a**
	Having explored the elements writers use in different genres, I can use what I learn to compose my own stories, poems and plays with interesting structures, characters and/or settings. **ENG 1-31a**

National Curriculum for Wales matching chart: Year 3

AT1 Oracy	Key Stage 2 Skills and Range	1	2	3	4	5	6	7	8	9	10	A	11	12	13	14	15	16	17	18	19	20	B
SKILLS: Pupils should be given opportunities to:	1. listen and view attentively, responding to a wide range of communication		✓		✓	✓					✓			✓					✓	✓	✓		
	2. identify key points and follow up ideas through question and comment, developing response to others in order to learn through talk	✓	✓	✓	✓			✓		✓			✓	✓			✓		✓	✓	✓		
	3. communicate clearly and confidently, expressing opinions, adapting talk to audience and purpose, using appropriate gesture, intonation and register in order to engage the listener	✓		✓		✓	✓	✓	✓	✓	✓					✓	✓	✓				✓	
	4. develop their awareness of the social conventions of conversation and discussion	✓	✓	✓	✓	✓	✓	✓	✓	✓	✓		✓	✓	✓	✓	✓	✓	✓	✓	✓	✓	
	5. develop their ability to use a range of sentence structures and vocabulary with precision, including terminology that allows them to discuss their work	✓	✓	✓	✓	✓	✓	✓	✓	✓	✓		✓	✓	✓	✓	✓		✓	✓	✓	✓	
	6. develop their understanding of when it is necessary to use standard English, and use formal and informal language appropriately			✓					✓										✓				
	7. evaluate their own and others' talk and drama activities and develop understanding of how to improve, considering how speakers adapt their vocabulary, tone, pace and style to suit a range of situations.										✓					✓							

continued overleaf

RANGE: Pupils should be given opportunities to develop their oral skills through:
1. seeing and hearing different people talking, including people with different dialects
2. experiencing and responding to a variety of stimuli and ideas: visual, audio and written
3. communicating for a range of purposes, e.g. presenting information, expressing opinions, explaining ideas, questioning, conveying feelings, persuading
4. speaking and listening individually, in pairs in groups and as members of a class
5. using a variety of methods to present ideas, including ICT, e.g. drama approaches, discussion and debate
6. presenting, talking and performing for a variety of audiences
7. increasing their confidence in language use by drawing on their knowledge of English, Welsh and other languages
8. engaging in activities that focus on words, their derivation, meanings, choice and impact.

National Curriculum for Wales matching chart: Year 3 *continued*

AT2 Reading

Key Stage 2 Skills and Range	1	2	3	4	5	6	7	8	9	10	A	11	12	13	14	15	16	17	18	19	20	B
SKILLS: Pupils should be given opportunities to:																						
1. develop phonic, graphic and grammatical knowledge, word recognition and contextual understanding within a balanced and coherent programme	✓	✓	✓	✓	✓	✓	✓	✓	✓	✓	✓	✓	✓	✓	✓	✓	✓	✓	✓	✓	✓	✓
2. develop their ability to read with fluency, accuracy, understanding and enjoyment	✓	✓	✓	✓	✓	✓	✓	✓	✓	✓	✓	✓	✓	✓	✓	✓	✓	✓	✓	✓	✓	✓
3. read in different ways for different purposes, including: • skimming, scanning and detailed reading • using prediction, inference and deduction • distinguishing between fact and opinion, bias and objectivity in what they read/view	✓	✓	✓	✓	✓	✓	✓	✓	✓	✓			✓	✓	✓	✓	✓	✓	✓	✓	✓	✓
4. recognise and understand the characteristics of different genres in terms of language, structure and presentation	✓	✓	✓	✓			✓				✓	✓		✓	✓	✓	✓	✓		✓		
5. consider what they read/view, responding orally and in writing to the ideas, vocabulary, style, presentation and organisation of image and language, and be able to select evidence to support their views	✓	✓				✓		✓		✓	✓	✓	✓		✓	✓	✓	✓	✓	✓	✓	✓
6a. use a range of appropriate information retrieval strategies including ICT. *e.g. the alphabet, indexes and catalogues*					✓		✓							✓		✓				✓		
6b. retrieve and collate information and ideas from a range of sources including printed, visual, audio, media, ICT and drama in performance		✓	✓															✓				

7. use the knowledge gained from reading to develop their understanding of the structure, vocabulary, grammar and punctuation of English, and of how these clarify meaning	✓
8. consider how texts change when they are adapted for different media and audiences.	✓
RANGE: Pupils should be given opportunities to develop their reading/viewing skills through:	
1. becoming enthusiastic and reflective readers	✓
2. reading individually and collaboratively	✓
3. experiencing and responding to a wide range of texts that include: • information, reference and other non-literary texts, including print, media, moving image and computer-based materials • poetry, prose and drama, both traditional and contemporary • texts with a Welsh dimension and texts from other cultures	✓
4. reading/viewing extracts and complete texts: • with challenging subject matter that broadens perspectives and extends thinking, e.g. environmental issues, sustainability, animal rights, healthy eating • with a variety of structural and organisational features • that show quality and variety in language use • that reflect the diversity of society in the twenty-first century • that reflect individual pupils' personal choice of reading matter.	✓

continued overleaf

National Curriculum for Wales matching chart: Year 3 *continued*

AT3 Writing	Key Stage 2 Skills and Range	1	2	3	4	5	6	7	8	9	10	A	11	12	13	14	15	16	17	18	19	20	B
SKILLS: Pupils should be given opportunities to communicate in writing to:	1. use the characteristic features of literary and non-literary texts in their own writing, adapting their style to suit the audience and purpose	✓	✓	✓			✓	✓				✓	✓		✓	✓	✓	✓	✓	✓		✓	
	2. use a range of sentence structures, linking them coherently and developing the ability to use paragraphs effectively			✓	✓		✓	✓	✓	✓	✓			✓		✓			✓	✓		✓	✓
	3. use punctuation to clarify meaning including full stop, exclamation and question marks, comma, apostrophe, bullet points, speech marks	✓					✓	✓	✓	✓	✓	✓	✓			✓				✓	✓	✓	
	4. choose and use appropriate vocabulary		✓										✓	✓				✓			✓		
	5. use the standard forms of English: nouns, pronouns, adjectives, adverbs, prepositions, connectives and verb tenses	✓					✓																
	6. develop and use a variety of strategies to enable them to spell correctly	✓	✓	✓	✓	✓	✓	✓	✓	✓	✓	✓	✓	✓	✓	✓	✓	✓	✓	✓	✓	✓	✓
	7. use appropriate vocabulary and terminology to consider and evaluate their own work and that of others					✓																	

	8. draft and improve their work, using ICT as appropriate, to: • plan • draft • revise • proof-read • prepare a final copy	9. present writing appropriately: • developing legible handwriting • using appropriate features of layout and presentation, including ICT	1. writing for a range of purposes, e.g. to entertain, report, inform, instruct, explain, persuade, recount, describe, imagine and to generate ideas	2. writing for a range of real or imagined audiences	3. writing in a range of forms	4. writing in response to a wide range of stimuli: visual, audio and written.
		✓			✓	✓
		✓	✓		✓	
		✓	✓		✓	
	✓	✓	✓	✓	✓	✓
	✓	✓	✓		✓	✓
	✓	✓	✓			✓
		✓	✓	✓		✓
		✓	✓	✓		✓
	✓	✓	✓			✓
	✓	✓	✓	✓	✓	✓
		✓			✓	✓
		✓	✓			
		✓	✓	✓	✓	✓
		✓	✓	✓	✓	
	✓	✓	✓		✓	
	✓	✓	✓		✓	✓
	✓	✓	✓			✓
	✓	✓	✓		✓	

RANGE:
Pupils should be given opportunities to improve and extend their writing through:

33

Revised Northern Ireland Curriculum matching chart: Year 4

Talking and Listening	1	2	3	4	5	6	7	8	9	10	A	11	12	13	14	15	16	17	18	19	20	B
participate in talking and listening in every area of learning	✓			✓	✓	✓	✓	✓		✓		✓			✓		✓					
listen to, respond to and explore stories, poems, songs, drama, and media texts through the use of traditional and digital resources and recreate parts of them in a range of expressive activities						✓				✓					✓							
listen to, interpret and retell, with some supporting detail, a range of oral and written texts									✓					✓								
tell their own stories based on personal experiences and imagination	✓		✓			✓		✓	✓	✓				✓		✓	✓					
listen to and respond to guidance and instructions	✓													✓		✓						
take turns at talking and listening in group and paired activities	✓		✓	✓	✓		✓	✓				✓					✓					
take part in a range of drama activities to support activity based learning across the curriculum										✓					✓							
express thoughts, feelings and opinions in response to personal experiences, imaginary situations, literature, media and curricular topics and activities	✓	✓	✓		✓		✓	✓	✓	✓		✓			✓	✓		✓	✓	✓	✓	
present ideas and information with some structure and sequence			✓					✓										✓				
think about what they say and how they say it			✓					✓										✓				
speak audibly and clearly, using appropriate quality of speech and voice			✓					✓		✓					✓			✓				
devise and ask questions to find information in social situations and across the curriculum			✓				✓													✓		
read aloud from a variety of sources, including their own work, inflecting appropriately to emphasise meaning		✓		✓									✓		✓		✓					
recognise and talk about features of spoken language, showing phonological awareness		✓		✓													✓					

Reading	1	2	3	4	5	6	7	8	9	10	A	11	12	13	14	15	16	17	18	19	20	B
participate in modelled, shared, paired and guided reading activities	✓	✓	✓	✓	✓	✓	✓	✓	✓	✓	✓	✓	✓	✓	✓	✓	✓	✓	✓	✓	✓	✓
read, and be read to from a wide selection of poetry and prose		✓		✓													✓					
read with some independence for enjoyment and information	✓	✓	✓	✓	✓	✓	✓	✓	✓	✓	✓	✓	✓	✓	✓	✓	✓	✓	✓	✓	✓	✓
read, explore, understand and make use of a range of traditional and digital texts	✓	✓	✓					✓							✓			✓		✓		
retell, re-read and act out a range of texts, representing ideas through drama, pictures, diagrams and ICT	✓			✓			✓							✓			✓					
begin to locate, select and use texts for specific purposes			✓		✓																	
research and manage information relevant to specific purposes, using traditional and digital sources, and present their findings in a variety of ways	✓	✓						✓								✓		✓		✓		
use a range of comprehension skills, both oral and written, to interpret and discuss texts	✓	✓	✓		✓	✓	✓		✓	✓	✓	✓	✓	✓	✓	✓	✓	✓	✓	✓	✓	✓
explore and begin to understand how texts are structured in a range of genres	✓	✓		✓	✓	✓	✓	✓	✓	✓	✓	✓	✓	✓		✓		✓	✓		✓	✓
explore and interpret a range of visual texts	✓		✓		✓			✓						✓		✓				✓		
express opinions and give reasons based on what they have read	✓	✓		✓	✓	✓	✓	✓	✓	✓	✓	✓	✓	✓	✓	✓	✓	✓	✓	✓	✓	✓
begin to use evidence from text to support their views	✓	✓		✓	✓	✓	✓	✓	✓	✓	✓	✓	✓	✓	✓	✓	✓	✓	✓	✓	✓	✓
read and share their own books of stories and poems including the use of digital resources					✓																	
build up a sight vocabulary								✓				✓	✓		✓							
use a range of strategies to identify unfamiliar words		✓		✓				✓				✓	✓		✓							
talk with the teacher about ways in which language is written down, identifying phrases, words, patterns or letters and other features of written language		✓		✓									✓			✓	✓					
recognise and notice how words are constructed and spelt		✓		✓				✓				✓			✓							

continued overleaf

Revised Northern Ireland Curriculum matching chart: Year 4 *continued*

Writing	1	2	3	4	5	6	7	8	9	10	A	11	12	13	14	15	16	17	18	19	20	B
participate in modelled, shared, guided and independent writing, including composing on-screen	✓	✓	✓					✓		✓									✓	✓		
understand and use a range of vocabulary by investigating and experimenting with language				✓							✓				✓		✓					
talk about and plan what they are going to write	✓	✓			✓					✓			✓		✓	✓	✓		✓			
begin to check their work in relation to specific criteria			✓			✓	✓											✓	✓		✓	
write without prompting, making their own decisions about form and content		✓				✓	✓				✓	✓		✓	✓	✓	✓	✓		✓	✓	✓
write for a variety of purposes and audiences	✓		✓			✓	✓				✓	✓	✓	✓		✓	✓	✓	✓			
express thoughts, feelings and opinions in imaginative and factual writing	✓		✓		✓		✓		✓	✓	✓	✓	✓	✓	✓	✓	✓	✓		✓		✓
organise, structure and present ideas and information using traditional and digital means	✓			✓		✓				✓	✓	✓		✓	✓	✓	✓					
understand some of the differences between spoken and written language		✓		✓						✓					✓							
use a variety of skills to spell words in their writing	✓	✓	✓	✓	✓	✓	✓	✓	✓	✓	✓	✓	✓	✓	✓	✓	✓	✓	✓	✓	✓	✓
spell correctly a range of familiar, important and regularly occurring words	✓	✓	✓	✓	✓	✓	✓	✓	✓	✓	✓	✓	✓	✓	✓	✓	✓	✓	✓	✓	✓	✓
develop increasing competence in the use of grammar and punctuation	✓	✓	✓	✓	✓	✓	✓	✓	✓	✓	✓	✓	✓	✓	✓	✓	✓	✓	✓	✓	✓	✓
develop a swift and legible style of handwriting	✓	✓	✓	✓	✓	✓	✓	✓	✓	✓	✓	✓	✓	✓	✓	✓	✓	✓	✓	✓	✓	✓

International matching chart

Unit	Cambridge International Primary Programme Primary English Curriculum Framework Stage 3 Objectives	International Baccalaureate Primary Years Programme Transdisciplinary Themes	World Class Learning International Primary Curriculum Milepost 2 Themes
1 Monkey Business *Non-fiction: reports*	**Reading** • scan a passage to find specific information and answer questions • consider ways that information is set out **Writing** • write first-person accounts and descriptions **Speaking and listening** • take turns in discussion, building on what others have said • listen and respond appropriately to other views and opinions	Sharing the planet	Saving the world (Rainforests) Do you live around here? (Habitats)
2 Caterpillars *Poetry: language play*	**Reading** • read aloud with expression to engage the listener • practice reading and reciting poems **Writing** • write portraits of characters • write and perform poems, attending to the sound of words **Speaking and listening** • take turns in discussion, building on what others have said • listen and respond appropriately to other views and opinions	Sharing the planet	Do you live around here? (Habitats)
3 Working on a Farm *Non-fiction: information texts*	**Reading** • consider ways that information is set out **Writing** • write portraits of characters **Speaking and listening** • take turns in discussion, building on what others have said • listen and respond appropriately to other views and opinions	How the world works	Food and farming (Survival) How does it work? (Inventions and machines)

continued overleaf

International matching chart *continued*

Unit	Cambridge International Primary Programme Primary English Curriculum Framework Stage 3 Objectives	International Baccalaureate Primary Years Programme Transdisciplinary Themes	World Class Learning International Primary Curriculum Milepost 2 Themes
4 The Cow *Poetry: language play*	**Reading** • read aloud with expression to engage the listener • practice reading and reciting poems **Writing** • write portraits of characters • write and perform poems, attending to the sound of words **Speaking and listening** • take turns in discussion, building on what others have said • listen and respond appropriately to other views and opinions	Sharing the planet	Do you live around here? (Habitats)
5 Looking at Books *Non-fiction: information texts*	**Reading** • work out what a book is about from skimming its main features **Writing** • write book reviews summarising what the book is about **Speaking and listening** • take turns in discussion, building on what others have said • listen and respond appropriately to other views and opinions	How the world works	Paintings, pictures and photographs (Visual representation)
6 Gumdrop Has a Birthday *Narrative: stories with familiar settings; significant authors*	**Reading** • begin to infer meanings beyond the literal (eg. about motives and character) **Writing** • write letters, notes and messages **Speaking and listening** • take turns in discussion, building on what others have said • listen and respond appropriately to other views and opinions	How we express ourselves	Young and old (People of different ages)
7 An Ants' Nest *Non-fiction: information texts*	**Reading** • scan a passage to find specific information and answer questions • consider ways that information is set out **Writing** • make a record of information drawn from a text (eg. by filling a chart) **Speaking and listening** • take turns in discussion, building on what others have said • listen and respond appropriately to other views and opinions	How we organise ourselves	Do you live around here? (Habitats)

continued overleaf

Unit	Objectives		
8 Thunder and Lightning *Narrative: myths and legends*	**Reading** • begin to infer meanings beyond the literal (eg. about motives and character) **Writing** • begin to organise writing in paragraphs in extended stories **Speaking and listening** • take turns in discussion, building on what others have said • listen and respond appropriately to other views and opinions	How we express ourselves	Living together (Community)
9 The Lion and the Mouse *Narrative: myths and legends; significant authors*	**Reading** • begin to infer meanings beyond the literal (eg. about motives and character) **Writing** • begin to organise writing in paragraphs in extended stories **Speaking and listening** • take turns in discussion, building on what others have said • listen and respond appropriately to other views and opinions	Sharing the planet	Living together (Community)
10 The Dragon's Cold *Narrative: stories with familiar settings*	**Reading** • begin to infer meanings beyond the literal (eg. about motives and character) **Writing** • write first-person accounts and descriptions based on observation • write simple playscripts, based on reading **Speaking and listening** • take turns in discussion, building on what others have said • listen and respond appropriately to other views and opinions	Who we are	Living together (Community) Health and fitness
Progress Unit A Crash! *Narrative: adventure and mystery*	**Reading** • begin to infer meanings beyond the literal (eg. about motives and character) **Writing** • plan main points as a structure for story writing	How we express ourselves	Living together (Community)

International matching chart continued

Unit	Cambridge International Primary Programme Primary English Curriculum Framework Stage 3 Objectives	International Baccalaureate Primary Years Programme Transdisciplinary Themes	World Class Learning International Primary Curriculum Milepost 2 Themes
11 Fun on Bikes *Non-fiction: information texts*	**Reading** • consider ways that information is set out • consider words that make an impact (eg. adjectives and powerful verbs) **Speaking and listening** • take turns in discussion, building on what others have said • listen and respond appropriately to other views and opinions	How we organise ourselves	Health and fitness
12 The Owl Who Was Afraid of the Dark *Narrative: stories with familiar settings; significant authors*	**Reading** • begin to infer meanings beyond the literal (eg. about motives and character) • practice reading and reciting poems **Writing** • begin to organise writing in paragraphs in extended stories **Speaking and listening** • take turns in discussion, building on what others have said • listen and respond appropriately to other views and opinions	Who we are	Do you live around here? (Habitats)
13 Lost in the Zoo *Non-fiction: instructions*	**Reading** • consider ways that information is set out **Speaking and listening** • take turns in discussion, building on what others have said • listen and respond appropriately to other views and opinions	Where we are in place and time	Explorers and adventurers
14 The Tale of Peter Rabbit *Narrative: stories with familiar settings; significant authors*	**Reading** • begin to infer meanings beyond the literal (eg. about motives and character) **Writing** • write first-person accounts and descriptions based on observation • write simple playscripts, based on reading **Speaking and listening** • take turns in discussion, building on what others have said • listen and respond appropriately to other views and opinions	Sharing the planet	Do you live around here? (Habitats)

continued overleaf

	Reading / Writing / Speaking and listening		
15 On Holiday *Non-fiction: instructions*	**Reading** • consider ways that information is set out **Speaking and listening** • take turns in discussion, building on what others have said • listen and respond appropriately to other views and opinions	How we organise ourselves	Living together (Community)
16 Roger the Dog *Poetry: language play; significant authors*	**Reading** • read aloud with expression to engage the listener • practice reading and reciting poems **Writing** • write portraits of characters • write and perform poems, attending to the sound of words **Speaking and listening** • take turns in discussion, building on what others have said • listen and respond appropriately to other views and opinions • practice to improve performance when reading aloud	Sharing the planet	Do you live around here? (Habitats)
17 Gran's New House *Narrative: letters*	**Reading** • consider ways that information is set out • scan a passage to find specific information and answer questions **Writing** • write letters, notes and messages **Speaking and listening** • take turns in discussion, building on what others have said • listen and respond appropriately to other views and opinions	How we express ourselves	Young and old (People of different ages)
18 Hot Dog Harris *Narrative: stories with familiar settings; significant authors*	**Reading** • begin to infer meanings beyond the literal (eg. about motives and character) **Writing** • write portraits of characters • make a record of information drawn from a text **Speaking and listening** • take turns in discussion, building on what others have said • listen and respond appropriately to other views and opinions	Sharing the planet	Living together (Community)

International matching chart *continued*

Unit	Cambridge International Primary Programme Primary English Curriculum Framework Stage 3 Objectives	International Baccalaureate Primary Years Programme Transdisciplinary Themes	World Class Learning International Primary Curriculum Milepost 2 Themes
19 Funny Feeders *Non-fiction: information texts*	**Reading** • scan a passage to find specific information and answer questions • locate information in non-fiction texts using contents page and index **Writing** • make a record of information drawn from a text **Speaking and listening** • take turns in discussion, building on what others have said • listen and respond appropriately to other views and opinions	How the world works	Do you live around here? (Habitats)
20 Mrs Wobble the Waitress *Narrative: stories with familiar settings; significant authors*	**Reading** • begin to infer meanings beyond the literal (eg. about motives and character) **Writing** • write portraits of characters **Speaking and listening** • take turns in discussion, building on what others have said • listen and respond appropriately to other views and opinions	How we express ourselves	Living together (Community)
Progress Unit B The Golly Sisters Go West *Narrative: dialogue and plays; significant authors*	**Reading** • begin to infer meanings beyond the literal (eg. about motives and character) **Writing** • use reading as a model for writing dialogue	Sharing the planet	Living together (Community)

Unit by unit question types

Unit	Do you remember?	More to think about	Now try these
1 Monkey Business	word selection	literal and deductive answering in sentences	character empathy
2 Caterpillars	word selection	literal and deductive answering in sentences; vocabulary work	vocabulary work; simple imagery
3 Working on a Farm	word selection	sentence completion; literal answers	empathy – likes/dislikes; conveying information
4 The Cow	selecting sentence endings	selecting true sentences; rhyme	evaluating statements; vocabulary work
5 Looking at Books	cloze	deductive answering	referencing; evaluating
6 Gumdrop Has a Birthday	literal responses	assessing true/false/probably/can't tell	deduction; character empathy
7 An Ants' Nest	cloze from passage	deductive answering in sentences; collating factual statements	empathy; lists – assessing and evaluating
8 Thunder and Lightning	word selection	sentence sequencing; vocabulary work	incident empathy; inference; word work
9 The Lion and the Mouse	cloze from passage	assessing true/false/can't tell; sentence sequencing	emotional empathy
10 The Dragon's Cold	word selection	literal and deductive answering in sentences	prediction; lists – assessing and evaluating; character empathy
Progress Unit A Crash!	cloze	writing sentences; interpreting pictures; character empathy	sequencing
11 Fun on Bikes	selecting sentence endings	deductive answering in sentences; vocabulary enrichment	emotional response; conveying information
12 The Owl Who Was Afraid of the Dark	selecting correct answers	deduction; vocabulary enrichment	interpreting language; summarising
13 Lost in the Zoo	cloze from passage	interpreting map	character empathy; conveying information
14 The Tale of Peter Rabbit	finishing sentences	deductive answering in sentences; vocabulary work	incident empathy; prediction
15 On Holiday	cloze from passage	deductive answering in sentences; figurative language	evaluating statements; conveying information
16 Roger the Dog	word selection	interpreting language	character empathy; expressing reasons; simple verse writing
17 Gran's New House	cloze from passage	deductive answering in sentences; correcting sentence content	imaginative description; evaluating; conveying information
18 Hot Dog Harris	cloze from passage	correcting sentence content; deductive answering in sentences	character empathy; imaginative description
19 Funny Feeders	cloze from passage	deductive answering in sentences	character empathy; imaginative description
20 Mrs Wobble the Waitress	reversing sentences	working with phrases; deductive answering in sentences	summarising; outcome prediction; critical evaluation of content
Progress Unit B The Golly Sisters Go West	cloze	correcting sentence content; deductive answering in sentences	summary; inference; prediction; empathy

Monkey Business

Planning

- **Learning objectives**
  7: Identify and make notes of the main points of section(s) of text
  8: Empathise with characters and debate moral dilemmas portrayed in texts
  1: Sustain conversation, explain or give reasons for their views or choices
  2: Follow up others' points and show whether they agree or disagree in whole-class discussion
  9: Write non-narrative texts using structures of different text-types

- **Cross-curricular links**
  Citizenship: in the media – what's the news?
  Science: plants and animals in the local environment

- **Assessing Pupils' Progress**
  Reading: AF1, AF2, AF3, AF4
  Writing: AF2, AF3, AF6
  Speaking and listening: AF1, AF2

  CPL Pupil Book 3 Unit 3

Vocabulary

latch – closing mechanism on door
irate – cross, annoyed

Introduction

Overview

This is a newspaper article reporting an incident on a motorway when a lorry-load of chimpanzees escape.

Before you read

- **SL: AF2**

Discuss the children's experiences of travelling in vehicles on major roads. Talk about the long periods of boredom and frustration at being confined in a car or coach.

If available, show the children pictures of chimpanzees and talk about how they are very advanced mammals with many similarities to humans.

Answers

Do you remember?

Word selection

- **R: AF1, AF2**

Copy these sentences. Choose the correct word to fill each gap.

1. The monkeys escaped from a *lorry*.
2. It was taking them to a *zoo*.
3. They got out through the *door*.
4. *Most* of the car drivers thought it was funny.
5. The police inspector called them *cheeky chimps*.

More to think about

Literal and deductive answering in sentences

- R: AF2, AF3; W: AF6

Write a sentence to answer each question.

1. Why did the lorry driver leave the monkeys on their own?
   The lorry had broken down so the driver went to get help.

2. Do you think the chimps were pleased to be out of the lorry? Why?
   I think the chimps thought it was great fun to be out of the lorry because they didn't like being stuck in the lorry.

3. How did the monkeys get out of the lorry?
   The chimps got out of the lorry by lifting the latch on the door.

4. Why were some of the drivers cross?
   Some of the drivers were cross because the chimps caused a traffic jam.

5. Write these phrases in your own words.
   a) some drivers got irate
   b) most drivers were prepared to see the funny side
   (Children's own answer.)

Now try these

Character empathy

- R: AF3; W: AF2, AF3

1. Imagine you are one of the monkeys. Write the article from your point of view.
   (Children's own answer.)

2. One of the drivers writes a letter to the zoo complaining about the incident. Pretend you are the driver and write the letter.
   (Children's own answer.)

3. Where do you think the monkeys would prefer to be: in the zoo, loose on the road or in the jungle? Explain your answer.
   (Children's own answer.)

Enrichment

- Ask individual children to describe an incident they might have seen on a motorway or major road. Encourage them not only to describe the event and its immediate effects, such as delays and disruption but also to explain how it made them feel. Encourage empathy towards those directly involved. (SL: AF1)

- Ask the children to put themselves in the place of a pet they might have and to explain to a partner the advantages and disadvantages of living with their owner. (SL: AF1)

- Provide clippings from local and national newspapers for the children to look through in groups. Ask them to discuss and give feedback on the content and layout features. (R: AF4, SL: AF2)

- Ask the children to put themselves in the place of a local reporter when a lorry transporting animals passes through their town. Use Resource Sheet 1B as a template for an article describing what happens when the lorry crashes and the animals (perhaps elephants, giraffes or lions) escape. (W: AF2, AF3)

 Resource Sheet 1A (R: AF3)

 Resource Sheet 1B (W: AF2, AF3)

Further reading

Simple stories about animals from the local and national newspapers.

Antarctica: Land of the Penguins by Jonathan and Angela Scott (Collins Big Cat, 2005);
Kings of the Wild by Jonathan and Angela Scott (Collins Big Cat, 2007).

Monkey Business

Name _____ **Date** _____

Write 'true', 'false' or 'can't tell' next to each of these sentences.

1. The monkeys escaped from a ship bringing them from Africa.

   _____

2. It was taking them to Burwell Zoo. _____

3. The chimps were all very hungry and thirsty. _____

4. They got out through the door. _____

5. One of the chimps broke the latch so they could get out.

   _____

6. All of the car drivers thought it was funny. _____

7. The monkeys all went and sat in the trees. _____

8. The police inspector called them cheeky chimps.

   _____

9. The road was reopened after three hours. _____

Unit 1B

Monkey Business

Name _____   **Date** _____

Pretend you are the reporter for the local newspaper.
You have talked to some people who saw what happened when some animals escaped.
Now you need to write a report.
Don't forget to start with a good headline.

Headline

From our reporter _____

_____

_____

_____

_____

_____

_____

Caterpillars

Poetry: language play

Planning

- **Learning objectives**
  - 7: Infer characters' feelings in fiction and consequences in logical explanations
  - 7: Explore how different texts appeal to readers using varied sentence structures and descriptive language
  - 8: Identify features that writers use to provoke readers' reactions
  - 1: Choose and prepare poems or stories for performance, identifying appropriate expression, tone, volume and use of voices and other sounds
  - 9: Write non-narrative texts using structures of different text-types
  - 9: Select and use a range of technical and descriptive vocabulary

- **Cross-curricular links**
  Science: plants and animals in the local environment; habitats; life cycles

- **Assessing Pupils' Progress**
  Reading: AF1, AF2, AF3, AF5
  Writing: AF1, AF6, AF7
  Speaking and listening: AF2, AF4

CPL Pupil Book 3 Unit 4

Introduction

Overview

This is a descriptive poem about caterpillars on a plant.

Before you read

SL: AF2

Talk about the caterpillar and its place in the life cycle of a butterfly.

Discuss why it is helpful for caterpillars to be a similar colour to the plant on which they live (camouflage). For example, Cabbage White butterflies lay eggs on green plants (such as cabbages) which hatch into green caterpillars.

Answers

Do you remember?

Word selection

- **R: AF1, AF2**

Copy these sentences. Choose the correct word to fill each gap.

1. The caterpillars look like *clowns*.
2. They are clinging to twigs with their *feet*.
3. They are looking for something to *eat*.
4. Caterpillars eat *leaves*.
5. *Green* is the most usual colour of caterpillars.

More to think about

> Literal and deductive answering in sentences; vocabulary work

- R: AF2, AF3, AF5; W: AF6

1. Write a sentence to answer each question.
   a) In what way are some caterpillars like circus clowns?
      Caterpillars are painted bright colours like circus clowns.
   b) Are all caterpillars smooth to touch?
      Not all caterpillars are smooth to touch.
      ***Notes:** The children might refer to the bristles some caterpillars have.*
   c) What different sorts of patterns do caterpillars have on their bodies?
      Some caterpillars have spots and some have patches like polka dots.
   d) Is it easier to spot a green or a blue caterpillar on a green leaf?
      It is easier to spot a blue caterpillar on a green leaf.
   e) Why is it better for caterpillars if they are hard to find?
      If caterpillars are hard to find they are more protected from danger/less likely to be attacked.

2. Match a word from each box to make pairs of words that have similar meanings. One has been done to help you.
   clinging = holding
   chewing = munching
   looking = searching
   dots = spots
   tiny = small

Now try these

> Vocabulary work; simple imagery

- R: AF2; AF5; W: AF7

1. Find a word in the poem that rhymes with:
   a) down: *clown*   b) feet: *eat*
   c) spots: *dots*   d) blue: *chew*

2. The poet says some caterpillars look like clowns. Make a list of anything else they remind you of.
   (Children's own answer.)

   ***Notes:** Children's answers should reflect colour, size or movement and other behavioural characteristics (such as voracious appetite) of the caterpillar.*

Enrichment

- Using books or, if available, electronic media, ask the children, in pairs, to research the life cycle of butterflies. Ask them to make a diagram to illustrate the various stages. (R: AF2)

- Give the children poetry anthologies to browse through in groups, to find other poems about butterflies, moths or other small creatures. Select a few children to read some aloud and ask the class to vote for the favourite. (SL: AF4)

- Ask the children to write a personal account of what it is like being a caterpillar. Resource Sheet 2B can be used to give structure to this activity, if appropriate. (W: AF1)

 Resource Sheet 2A (R: AF2)

 Resource Sheet 2B (W: AF1, AF7)

Further reading

Classic Poetry: An Illustrated Collection, selected by Michael Rosen (Walker Books, 2009);
I like this poem: a collection of best-loved poems, edited by Kaye Webb (Puffin, 2007);
The Oxford Book of Children's Poetry by Michael Harrison and Christopher Stuart-Clark (Oxford University Press, 2007);
Something's Drastic by Michael Rosen (Collins Big Cat, 2007);
Weird Little Monsters by Nic Bishop (Collins Big Cat, 2007).

Caterpillars

Name _____   **Date** _____

A. Read the poem again.
Close your book then try to remember the words that are missing in these sentences.

1. The caterpillars look like _____.

2. They are clinging to twigs with their _____.

3. They are always looking for something to _____.

4. Caterpillars eat mostly _____.

5. _____ is the most usual colour of caterpillars.

B. Look at the poem again.
Find the word that rhymes with each of these words.

down _____   feet _____

dots _____   chew _____

Caterpillars

Name _____ **Date** _____

1. Imagine that you are a caterpillar sitting on a plant on a sunny day. Write some words that describe where you are and what is happening around you.

_____ _____ _____

_____ _____ _____

_____ _____ _____

2. Use these words to help you write a few sentences for a diary entry. Describe your feelings and what happens when a bird lands nearby!

_____

_____

_____

_____

Working on a Farm

Planning

- **Learning objectives**
  - 7: Identify how different texts are organised, including reference texts, magazines and leaflets, on paper and on screen
  - 1: Sustain conversation, explain or give reasons for their views or choices
  - 2: Follow up others' points and show whether they agree or disagree in whole-class discussion
  - 9: Write non-narrative texts using structures of different text-types
  - 9: Use layout, format graphics and illustrations for different purposes

- **Cross-curricular links**
  Geography: a contrasting locality; investigating our local area
  History: what was it like to live here in the past?

- **Assessing Pupils' Progress**
  Reading: AF1, AF2, AF3
  Writing: AF2, AF3, AF6
  Speaking and listening: AF1, AF2

CPL Pupil Book 3 Unit 11

Introduction

Overview

This is a pictorial information unit about arable farming.

Before you read

- **SL: AF1, AF2**

Talk about where food comes from. Discuss the balance of people living in cities and towns compared to those living in the countryside who produce most of the raw materials that go to make our food.

Ask the children to volunteer their experiences if they have ever been on a farm.

Answers

Do you remember?

Word selection

- **R: AF1, AF2**

Copy these sentences. Choose the correct word to fill each gap.

1. In picture 1 the farmer is *ploughing*.
2. After ploughing, he *rakes* the soil.
3. The ground is now ready for sowing the *seed*.
4. The seed needs *rain* to help it grow.

More to think about

Sentence completion; literal answers

- R: AF3; W: AF6

1. Write a sentence to answer each question.
   a) What job is being done in picture 4?
      In picture 4 the farmer is harvesting.
   b) Which season does picture 4 show?
      Picture 4 shows a summer scene.

2. Copy the flow chart and fill in the boxes to show the process of farming.
   ploughing → raking the soil → sowing the seed → harvesting

Now try these

Empathy – likes/dislikes; conveying information

- W: AF2, AF3

1. Imagine you are a farmer. Copy and complete the table.

Things I **like** about being a farmer	Things I **dislike** about being a farmer
working outside in the sunshine	*working outside in the rain/cold*
being with animals	*cleaning out animals*
driving tractors	

Notes: *Encourage consideration of the pros and cons.*

2. Choose one of the pictures. Write Farmer Lindsay's diary entry about a day on the farm, using the picture to help you.
   (Children's own answer.)

Enrichment

- This unit of work focuses on arable farming. Encourage the children to research other forms of farming both in their own country and abroad. Ask them to prepare a presentation in groups to give to the rest of the class. (R: AF2; SL: AF1)

- Farming has been undertaken on the same land for hundreds, and sometimes thousands, of years. Ask the children to research and discuss how the farmers would have worked before modern-day machines were available. Select a specific period related to other work being undertaken for this comparison. (R: AF2; SL: AF2)

- The cycle of the year is reflected in pastoral as well as arable cultivation. Use Resource Sheet 3B to support the children in producing a similar set of labelled pictures illustrating, with captions, what is likely to be seen on a dairy or sheep farm. (W: AF2, AF3)

 Resource Sheet 3A (R: AF3; W: AF6)

 Resource Sheet 3B (W: AF2, AF3)

Further reading

A Visit to the Farm by Michael Morpurgo (Collins Big Cat, 2005);
From Farm to Table by Richard and Louise Spilsbury (Wayland, 2009);
Farming by Cassie Mayer and Lisa Easterling (Heinemann Library, 2008).

Working on a Farm

Name _____   **Date** _____

Write a sentence to say what is happening in each picture.

1. _____   2. _____

_____   _____

3. _____   4. _____

_____   _____

Working on a Farm

Name _____ **Date** _____

What happens on a dairy or a sheep farm?

A year on a _____ **farm**

1. _____

_____

2. _____

_____

3. _____

_____

4. _____

_____

The Cow

Planning

- **Learning objectives**
  7: Explore how different texts appeal to readers using varied sentence structures and descriptive language
  7: Infer characters' feelings in fiction and consequences in logical explanations
  8: Identify features that writers use to provoke readers' reactions
  1: Choose and prepare poems or stories for performance, identifying appropriate expression, tone, volume and use of voices and other sounds

- **Cross-curricular links**
  Science: habitats
  Citizenship: animals and us

- **Assessing Pupils' Progress**
  Reading: AF1, AF2, AF3, AF5, AF6
  Writing: AF2, AF3
  Speaking and listening: AF2, AF4

CPL Pupil Book 3 Unit 4

Vocabulary

lowing – sound a cow makes (mooing)

Introduction

Overview

This is a simple, descriptive poem about a dairy cow.

Before you read

- SL: AF2

Discuss how this unit follows on from the previous unit about farming. Talk about the difference between fiction and non-fiction genres.

Ensure that all children are fully aware of the source of milk – especially those who have little opportunity to visit or see the countryside.

Author biography

- **Robert Louis Stevenson** was born in Edinburgh, Scotland in 1850.

- He suffered chronic health problems as a child.

- He studied science at university.

- At 23 he became very ill and started writing.

- His most famous works, including *Treasure Island*, were written between 1880 and 1887.

- He died when he was only 44.

Answers

Do you remember?

Selecting sentence endings

- R: AF1, AF2

Copy these sentences. Choose the correct ending to finish each sentence.

1. The cow in the poem *a) is friendly*.

2. Her coat is *b) red and white*.

3. Some of her milk is made into *c) cream*.

4. She wanders about *b) making contented sounds*.

5. When it rains *a) she gets wet*.

More to think about

Selecting true sentences; rhyme

- R: AF2, AF3, AF5

1. Read these sentences about the poem. Write 'true' or 'not true' for each one.
   a) She likes to eat meadow flowers. *true*
   b) She keeps getting out of her field. *not true*
   c) She lives all day in a barn. *not true*
   d) She stays outside in the wind. *true*

2. Find words in the poem that rhyme with the following words:
   a) might: *white*
   b) there: *air*
   c) heart: *tart*
   d) flowers: *showers*

Now try these

Evaluating statements; vocabulary work

- R: AF3, AF5, AF6

1. Think carefully about these questions. Write sentences to answer each one.
   a) Do you think the poet owns the cow? Explain your answer.
      The poet probably owns the cow as he uses her cream.
   b) The poet mentions the cream given by the cow. What other reasons might he have for loving her?
      Children may refer here to the friendliness of the cow and other character traits.
   c) What word does the poet use to make you know he likes the outdoor life?
      pleasant

2. Find these words in the poem. Explain what they mean in your own words.
   a) with all my heart: *for example, a lot, deeply, enormously*
   b) with all her might: *for example, to the best of her ability*
   c) pleasant: *for example, enjoyable, agreeable*

Enrichment

- Discuss why the cow is such an important creature for us. Ask the children, in pairs, to list all the different foodstuffs that come from dairy farming. (SL: AF2)

- Talk about the importance of dairy products in our diets. Ask the children to draw a pie diagram or pyramid diagram showing the different food groups that make up our diet. (W: AF3)

- Give the children poetry anthologies to browse through in groups to find other poems about cows and/or farming. Select a few children to read some aloud and ask the class to vote for the favourite. (SL: AF4)

- Ask the children to read the poem again and then write an account of what it would be like being a cow. Discuss the good and bad points before they start. Resource Sheet 4B supports this activity. (R: AF3, W: AF2)

 Resource Sheet 4A (R: AF2)

 Resource Sheet 4B (R: AF3, W: AF2)

Further reading

Classic Poetry: An Illustrated Collection, selected by Michael Rosen (Walker Books, 2009);
I like this poem: a collection of best-loved poems, edited by Kaye Webb (Puffin, 2007);
The Oxford Book of Children's Poetry by Michael Harrison and Christopher Stuart-Clark (Oxford University Press, 2007).

Websites for 'cow' poems:
www.kiddyhouse.com/Farm/Cows/
www.blackcatpoems.com/c/cow_poems

The Cow

Name _____   Date _____

A. Write 'true' or 'not true' next to each of these sentences.

1. The cow in the poem is friendly.   _____

The cow in the poem is aggressive.   _____

2. Her coat is red and white.   _____

Her coat is black and white.   _____

3. Some of her milk is made into cheese.   _____

Some of her milk is made into cream.   _____

4. She wanders about in silence.   _____

She wanders about making contented sounds.   _____

5. When it rains she gets wet.   _____

When it rains she keeps dry under the trees.   _____

B. Find a word in the poem that rhymes with each of these words.

white   _____   heart   _____

there   _____   stray   _____

grass   _____   flowers   _____

The Cow

Name _____ **Date** _____

Write five good things and five bad things about being a cow.

Good things about being a cow	Bad things about being a cow
1.	1.
2.	2.
3.	3.
4.	4.
5.	5.

Having thought about it carefully I have decided that
I **would/wouldn't** (*cross one out*) like to be a cow mainly because

_____

_____

_____

Unit 5 Looking at Books

Planning

- **Learning objectives**
  7: Identify how different texts are organised, including reference texts, magazines and leaflets, on paper and on screen
  8: Share and compare reasons for reading preferences, extending the range of books read
  1: Sustain conversation, explain or give reasons for their views or choices
  1: Develop and use specific vocabulary in different contexts
  2: Follow up others' points and show whether they agree or disagree in whole-class discussion
  3: Actively include and respond to all members of the group
  9: Select and use a range of technical and descriptive vocabulary

- **Cross-curricular links**
  Design and technology: storybooks

- **Assessing Pupils' Progress**
  Reading: AF1, AF2, AF3, AF4
  Writing: AF2
  Speaking and listening: AF1, AF2

CPL Pupil Book 3 Unit 11

Introduction

Overview

This illustrative text provides a way of exploring the value of book covers in giving guidance to the contents.

Before you read

- **SL: AF2**

Select a range of books and discuss how the contents can, or can't, be deduced from examining the covers.

Discuss the purpose of a few book covers and ask the children to explain why they do or do not find them appropriate or appealing.

Answers

Do you remember?

Cloze

- **R: AF1, AF2**

Copy these sentences. Choose words from the box to fill each gap.

1. The title of the book is *Keeping Small Animals*.

2. The author of the book is called *James Matthews*.

3. An author is the person who *writes* the words.

4. The name of the illustrator of the book is *Sarah Richards*.

5. An illustrator is the person who *draws* the pictures.

More to think about

- R: AF2, AF3

Look at these book covers. Write numbers to answer each question.

1. Which is the story book? *1*

2. In which book could I check the meaning of a word? *4*

3. Which book did Hilary Frost write? *3*

4. In which book might I find facts about elephants? *2*

5. Which book will help me check the spelling of a word? *4*

6. Which book might tell me about the River Amazon? *3*

7. Which of the books was written by Kenneth Grahame? *1*

8. In which two books might I discover more about where alligators live? *2 and 3*

Now try these

Referencing; evaluating

- R: AF2, AF4; W: AF2

1. Write the title and author of one of each of these types of books that you can find in your classroom. Some of the books you choose might have more than one author.

   A book that:
   a) tells you about birds
   b) has a story
   c) helps you with spelling words
   d) has lots of pictures
   e) is about another country
   f) is your favourite
   (Children's own answer.)

   Notes: *This activity lends itself to early discussions on the merits of individual books, and gives an opportunity for the expression of opinions.*

2. Write a book review of a book you have read recently. Remember to explain why you liked or disliked it.
   (Children's own answer.)

Enrichment

- Give groups of children a small selection of books. Invite each group to select the book with the cover that appeals most to them, explaining their reasons. Then ask them to select the book with the cover that appeals least to them, explaining their reasons. (SL: AF1, AF2)

- Ask the children to write some simple book reviews, using Resource Sheet 5B as a template if appropriate. (W: AF2)

 Resource Sheet 5A (R: AF2)

 Resource Sheet 5B (W: AF2)

Further reading

How to make Storybooks by Ros Asquith (Collins Big Cat, 2005);
Nick Butterworth: Making Books by Nick Butterworth (Collins Big Cat, 2005).

Looking at Books

Name _____ **Date** _____

Draw a line to the correct answer to finish each sentence.

Animals.

1. The title of the book is

Keeping Small Animals.

James Matthews.

2. The author of the book is

Sarah Richards.

writes the words.

3. An author is the person who

draws the pictures.

James Matthews.

4. The illustrator of the book is

Sarah Richards.

writes the words.

5. An illustrator is the person who

draws the pictures.

Looking at Books

Name _____   **Date** _____

My book review

Title of book _____

Name of author _____

Name of illustrator _____

Things I liked most about this book

_____

_____

_____

Things I didn't like about this book

_____

_____

Gumdrop Has a Birthday

Narrative: stories with familiar settings; significant authors

Planning

- **Learning objectives**
  - 7: Infer characters' feelings in fiction and consequences in logical explanations
  - 8: Empathise with characters and debate moral dilemmas portrayed in texts
  - 1: Sustain conversation, explain or give reasons for their views or choices
  - 2: Follow up others' points and show whether they agree or disagree in whole-class discussion
  - 9: Write non-narrative texts using structures of different text-types

- **Cross-curricular links**
  History: how has life in Britain changed since 1948?

- **Assessing Pupils' Progress**
  Reading: AF1, AF2, AF3
  Writing: AF2, AF3
  Speaking and listening: AF1, AF2

CPL Pupil Book 3 Unit 1

Introduction

Overview

This text is about Gumdrop, a very old car that Mr Oldcastle has cherished for a long time. When Gumdrop reaches 50 years of age it seems only natural to celebrate his birthday.

Before you read

- **SL: AF2**

Talk about the value that we place on old and new things, and discuss the reasons behind our feelings.

Discuss whether there are any old items in the children's families that are especially valued.

Author biography

- **Val Biro** was born Balint Stephen Biro in Budapest, Hungary in 1921.

- He enjoyed school, and from an early age found that he had the knack of drawing funny people.

- Val moved to England to study art in July 1939.

- He became a full-time illustrator.

- Most of Val's time was taken up designing book covers and doing work for the Radio Times.

- He wrote 37 books about Gumdrop.

Answers

Do you remember?

> Literal responses

- **R: AF1, AF2**

Write the correct answer to each question.

1. Whose birthday is it?
   a) It is Gumdrop's birthday.

2. What is Gumdrop?
   b) Gumdrop is an old car.

3. What is the name of Mr Oldcastle's dog?
   b) The dog's name is Horace.

More to think about

- R: AF2, AF3

Read these sentences about the story. Write 'true', 'false', 'probably' or 'can't tell' for each one.

1. Mr Oldcastle is very fond of Gumdrop. *probably/true*

2. Gumdrop is 50 years old. *true*

3. Mr Oldcastle is the most popular person in the village. *can't tell*

4. The birthday cake vanished. *true*

5. The cake had rolled under Gumdrop. *false*

6. Horace had eaten the cake. *true*

Now try these

- R: AF3; W: AF2

1. Mr Oldcastle invited his friends to Gumdrop's party. Write the party invitation using as many details as you can.
(*Children's own answer.*)

2. Imagine you are Horace. Tell the story of the birthday party from your point of view.
(*Children's own answer.*)

   Notes: *Children might consider how the party would appear from a lower level perspective, as well as from that of a dog who can't necessarily interpret the events that are going on.*

3. Do you think Mr Oldcastle would have swapped Gumdrop for a smart and shiny new car? Give your reasons.
(*Children's own answer.*)

Enrichment

- Pets, like Horace the dog, can sometimes cause problems. Ask the children, in groups, to share experiences of when a pet has done a funny thing or caused a difficult situation. (SL: AF2)

- From the extract it is clear how important Gumdrop is to Mr Oldcastle. One of the stories tells of when Mr Oldcastle had no money and had to sell Gumdrop to someone who didn't look after him very well. Ask the children to describe how he would have felt. (SL: AF1)

- Resource Sheet 6A lists randomly the instructions for making Gumdrop's birthday cake. Use this activity to give practice in sequencing information. You can then ask the children to write their own list of instructions for a game or an activity. (W: AF2, AF3)

 Resource Sheet 6A (W: AF3)

 Resource Sheet 6B (W: AF2, AF3)

Further reading

Other Gumdrop titles by Val Biro:
Gumdrop at Sea (Award Publications, 2004);
Gumdrop and the Elephant (Award Publications, 2004);
Gumdrop and the Dinosaur (Award Publications, 2004);
Gumdrop and the Secret Switches (Award Publications, 2004).

Gumdrop Has a Birthday

Name _____   **Date** _____

Here are the instructions for making Gumdrop's birthday cake.
They are in the wrong order.
Put a number next to each instruction to show the correct order.

☐ Stir the ingredients.

☐ Wash your hands.

☐ Put the ingredients in a bowl.

☐ Bake the mixture in the oven.

☐ Ice the cake and put on the candles.

☐ Go to the shop to buy the ingredients.

Gumdrop Has a Birthday

Name _____ **Date** _____

1. One of the Gumdrop stories tells of when Mr Oldcastle had no money and had to sell Gumdrop to someone who didn't look after him very well. Imagine that you have to give away something that means a lot to you. Write some words that might describe how you feel.

_____ _____ _____

_____ _____ _____

_____ _____ _____

2. Now use these words to help you write a letter to a friend explaining your feelings.

_____

_____

_____

_____

An Ants' Nest

Planning

- **Learning objectives**
  7: Identify and make notes of the main points of section(s) of text
  7: Identify how different texts are organised, including reference texts, magazines and leaflets, on paper and on screen
  1: Sustain conversation, explain or give reasons for their views or choices
  2: Follow up others' points and show whether they agree or disagree in whole-class discussion
  9: Write non-narrative texts using structures of different text-types

- **Cross-curricular links**
  Science: habitats; plants and animals in the local environment; life cycles

- **Assessing Pupils' Progress**
  Reading: AF1, AF2, AF3, AF4
  Writing: AF1, AF6
  Speaking and listening: AF2

CPL Pupil Book 3 Unit 11

Introduction

Overview

This is an information text with photographic illustration, organised with sub-headings.

Before you read

- SL: AF2

Discuss how ant colonies are organised with queens, males and workers. Mention parallels with the social arrangements in human societies, with different roles being performed by different people.

Answers

Do you remember?

Cloze from passage

- R: AF1, AF2

Copy these sentences. Fill each gap.

1. Inside an ants' nest is a mass of *tunnels* and rooms.

2. There are *three* types of ant.

3. The biggest ants are the *queens*.

4. *Worker* ants are the smallest.

5. A queen ant's main job is to lay the *eggs*.

More to think about

Deductive answering in sentences; collating factual statements

- R: AF2, AF3; W: AF6

1. Write a sentence to answer each question.
   a) What are the three types of ant?
      The three types of ant are the queens, the males and the workers.
   b) Which two types of ants have wings?
      Queen and male ants both have wings.
   c) Who looks after the young ants?
      The young ants are looked after by worker ants.
   d) Why do there need to be so many worker ants for each queen?
      The queen ants have hundreds of young and so many worker ants are needed to feed them all.

2. Find two facts for each type of ant to complete the table.

Queen ant	Male ant	Worker ant
live in one room of the nest	*have wings clean*	*keep the nest*
lay hundreds of eggs	*mate with a queen*	*collect the food*

Notes: *other answers could include:*

Queen ants – *are the biggest in the nest; have wings.*

Male ants – *are bigger than worker ants; are smaller than queen ants; die after mating.*

Worker ants – *are the smallest of the ants; don't have wings; feed the young ants; dig the rooms and tunnels; defend the nest.*

Now try these

Empathy; lists – assessing and evaluating

- R: AF3; W: AF1

1. Imagine you suddenly shrink, and become ant-sized. You explore an ants' nest. Write a report about what you find.
   (Children's own answer.)

2. Ants are tiny, but when they work together they can do things they couldn't manage by themselves. Write down five things you can do alone, and five things you can do only with other people to help.
   (Children's own answer.)

Notes: *Both assignments call for empathy with the situation, and can provide fruitful starting points for discussion and imaginative exploration before starting written work.*

Enrichment

- Discuss how the text has been organised, with a main title and sub-titles which help the reader go quickly to the section they want to read. In groups, the children can look at other information books to compare the layouts. (R: AF4)

- Use Resource Sheet 7B to support a discussion about the similarities and differences in the ways that ants and humans arrange their lives. You could link this discussion to historical periods being studied. (SL: AF2)

- Ask the children, in pairs, to make a list of the things that can be found out only by reading the passage and a list of those things that are only apparent from looking at the pictures that accompany the text. (R: AF2)

 Resource Sheet 7A (R: AF2)

 Resource Sheet 7B (R: AF3)

Further reading

The Life Cycle of an Ant by Hadley Dyer (Crabtree Publishing Co, 2006);
Inside an Ant Colony by Allan Fowler (Children's Press, 1998);
Weird Little Monsters by Nic Bishop (Collins Big Cat, 2007);
Gulliver's Travels by Jonathan Swift (Oxford University Press, 2008);
The Borrowers by Mary Norton (Puffin, 2003).

An Ants' Nest

Name _____   Date _____

A. Choose a word from the box to finish each sentence.

eggs	three	tunnels	queens	Worker

1. Inside an ants' nest is a mass of _____ and rooms.

2. There are _____ types of ant.

3. The biggest ants are the _____.

4. _____ ants are the smallest.

5. A queen ant's main job is to lay the _____.

B. Write the names of the three types of ant.

_____   _____   _____

How can you tell them apart?

_____

_____

An Ants' Nest

Name _____   **Date** _____

Make two lists to show how ants are similar to humans and how they are different.

Ways ants are similar to humans	Ways ants are different from humans

Thunder and Lightning

Planning

- **Learning objectives**
  7: Infer characters' feelings in fiction and consequences in logical explanations
  8: Empathise with characters and debate moral dilemmas portrayed in texts
  1: Sustain conversation, explain or give reasons for their views or choices
  2: Follow up others' points and show whether they agree or disagree in whole-class discussion
  3: Actively include and respond to all members of the group
  9: Use beginning, middle and end to write narratives in which events are sequenced logically and conflicts resolved

- **Cross-curricular links**
  Geography: weather around the world

- **Assessing Pupils' Progress**
  Reading: AF1, AF2, AF3, AF5, AF7
  Writing: AF1, AF3, AF6
  Speaking and listening: AF1, AF2, AF4

CPL Pupil Book 3 Unit 5

Introduction

Overview

This passage is a brief summary of an old Nigerian legend explaining the origin of thunder and lightning.

Before you read

- **SL: AF2**

Talk about thunder and lightning. Discuss the children's ideas about how it is formed.

Talk about how difficult the phenomenon is to explain, hence the different legends that have built up – this being one of them.

Answers

Do you remember?

Word selection

- **R: AF1, AF2**

Copy the answers to these questions. Choose the correct word to fill each gap.

1. Where did this legend come from?
   This legend came from *Nigeria*.

2. What were Thunder and Lightning?
   Thunder and Lightning were *sheep*.

3. What did Lightning do to the crops?
   Lightning *burnt* the crops.

4. Where did the village chief send them?
   The village chief sent them to live in the *sky*.

More to think about

- R: AF2, AF3

1. Read these sentences about the story. Copy them in the right order.
   The correct order is:
   Thunder and Lightning were two troublesome sheep.
   The villagers became very annoyed.
   Eventually the village chief could stand it no longer.
   He sent them away to live in the sky.
   Thunder still grumbled away in her loud, booming voice.
   Lightning still upsets the villagers.

   Notes: *The last two sentences are interchangeable.*

2. Copy these two lists of words. Draw lines to join words that have similar meanings. One has been done to help you.
   fed up → annoyed
   complain → object to
   banished → sent away
   eventually → in the end
   troublesome → naughty

Now try these

- R: AF3

1. Imagine that you were a villager in this legend. Write about what happened, what you did about it, and how you felt.
   (Children's own answer.)

   Notes: *In discussion, encourage children to consider different approaches to the problem, together with the advantages and disadvantages of each.*

2. What do you think Thunder says to Lightning when she shouts at him?
   (Children's own answer.)

3. Thunder and lightning are words which often go together. Make a list of other pairs of words. Two have been done to help you.
   fish and chips
   table and chair
   Other examples include: horse and carriage; salt and pepper; bucket and spade; knife and fork.

Enrichment

- Ask individual children to describe what their feelings are about thunderstorms, and whether they have particular stories in their families to explain the loud claps and the flashes of lightning. (SL: AF1)

- Ask the children, in pairs, to research the real cause of thunder and lightning and prepare a presentation to give to the rest of the class. (R: AF2; SL: AF1)

- Ask the children to browse through poetry anthologies to find and share weather related poems, especially those connected with storms. Discuss how storms are described in poetry. Ask, 'What are they compared with?' (R: AF5; SL: AF4)

- In groups, ask the children to research other legends from different cultures about the causes of thunder and lightning. Ask each group to choose their favourite and explain why they like it best. (R: AF7; SL: AF2)

- Ask the children to write their own legend to explain the cause of thunder and lightning. Collect the legends together to make a class anthology. (W: AF1, AF3)

 Resource Sheet 8A (R: AF2; W: AF6)

 Resource Sheet 8B (W: AF3)

Further reading

Thunder and Lightning by Cassie Mayer (Heinemann Library, 2007);
Living with Climate Change by Alison Sage (Collins Big Cat, 2009);
The Cloud Forest by Nic Bishop (Collins Big Cat, 2005).

Thunder and Lightning

Name _____ **Date** _____

Write a sentence to answer each question.

1. Where did this legend come from?

_____

_____

2. What type of animals were Thunder and Lightning?

_____

_____

3. What did Lightning do to the crops?

_____

_____

4. Where did the village chief send them?

_____

_____

5. How does Thunder still keep the villagers awake?

_____

_____

Thunder and Lightning

Name _____   Date _____

Write and draw the legend of Thunder and Lightning as a comic strip.

Unit 9 — The Lion and the Mouse

Narrative: myths and legends; significant authors

Planning

- **Learning objectives**
  - 7: Infer characters' feelings in fiction and consequences in logical explanations
  - 8: Empathise with characters and debate moral dilemmas portrayed in texts
  - 1: Sustain conversation, explain or give reasons for their views or choices
  - 2: Follow up others' points and show whether they agree or disagree in whole-class discussion
  - 3: Actively include and respond to all members of the group
  - 9: Use beginning, middle and end to write narratives in which events are sequenced logically and conflicts resolved

- **Cross-curricular links**
  Citizenship: choices

- **Assessing Pupils' Progress**
  Reading: AF1, AF2, AF3
  Writing: AF1, AF3, AF7
  Speaking and listening: AF1, AF2

CPL Pupil Book 3 Unit 5

Vocabulary

spare me – don't harm me
gnaw – chew, bite

Introduction

Overview

This is a condensed version of Aesop's fable in which the lion spares the mouse, which means that later the mouse can rescue him. All of Aesop's fables have a strong moral and use animals to demonstrate human behaviour.

Before you read

- SL: AF1, AF2

This is an opportunity to discuss the notion that it is not always the biggest and strongest that can get things done most effectively. Also, that showing concern for those weaker than oneself can sometimes be rewarding.

Ask the children to volunteer examples of when they have helped someone or been kind to someone.

Author biography

- **Aesop** is known for the genre of fables ascribed to him.

- He is thought to have been born a slave in the mid-sixth century BC in ancient Greece.

Answers

Do you remember?

Cloze from passage

- R: AF1, AF2

Copy these sentences. Fill each gap.

1. The lion was going to *crush* the mouse.

2. The mouse said he would only be a *tiny* mouthful.

3. Mouse said he might be able to *help* the lion some day.

4. Lion became trapped in a *hunter's net*.

5. The mouse helped free the lion by *gnawing* at the ropes.

More to think about

Assessing true/false/can't tell; sentence sequencing

- R: AF2, AF3

1. Read these sentences about the story. Write 'true', 'false' or 'can't tell' for each one.
   a) The mouse pulled the lion's tail to wake him. *false*
   b) The lion was angry. *true*
   c) He ate the little mouse. *false*
   d) When the lion was trapped the mouse released him. *true*
   e) The animals live in Africa. *can't tell*

2. Read these sentences about the story. Copy them in the right order.
   The correct order is:
   A little mouse woke a lion.
   The lion grabbed the mouse.
   The lion was going to eat the mouse.
   The mouse persuaded the lion to set him free.
   The lion was trapped in the forest.
   The mouse helped the lion to escape.

Now try these

Emotional empathy

- R: AF3; W: AF1

1. Have you ever been frightened by someone bigger than you? Write some sentences about what happened and how you felt.
   (Children's own answer.)

   Notes: *Children will need to use empathy to 'think themselves into' this situation and explore how they felt.*

2. Aesop's fables often have a moral. The moral of this story is: **Don't belittle little things.** Write what you think it means.
   (Children's own answer.)

Notes: *Both questions may be used to help the children think about bullying.*

Enrichment

- Individual children can describe a particularly frightening situation they recall in which they were threatened by someone bigger or stronger than themselves. (SL: AF1)

- Use the opportunity to discuss the subject of bullying. Ask the children to discuss, in groups, ways in which they can help prevent weaker children being bullied by stronger children or threatened by groups. (SL: AF2)

- Ask the children to write a modern version of the fable in which a weaker creature is spared, and then later comes to the rescue of the creature that showed mercy. (W: AF1, AF3)

 Resource Sheet 9A (R: AF2)

 Resource Sheet 9B (R: AF3; W: AF7)

Further reading

The Orchard Book of Aesop's Fables by Michael Morpurgo (Orchard, 2004);
Aesop's Fables for Children by Milo Winter (Dover, 2008).

The Lion and the Mouse

Name _____   **Date** _____

Read the story and look at the pictures.
Write 'true', 'false' or 'can't tell' for each of these sentences.

1. The mouse pulled the lion's tail to wake him. _____

2. The lion was angry. _____

3. He ate the little mouse. _____

4. The mouse was a girl. _____

5. The mouse made the lion laugh. _____

6. When the lion was trapped the mouse released him. _____

7. The lion then ate the mouse. _____

8. The animals live in Africa. _____

The Lion and the Mouse

Name _____   **Date** _____

1. Next to each character write words to describe them.

_____   _____

_____   _____

_____   _____

_____   _____

_____   _____

_____   _____

2. Write some sentences to describe each of the characters in the fable.

Lion _____

_____

_____

Mouse _____

_____

Unit 10

The Dragon's Cold

Planning

- **Learning objectives**
  7: Infer characters' feelings in fiction and consequences in logical explanations
  8: Empathise with characters and debate moral dilemmas portrayed in texts
  1: Sustain conversation, explain or give reasons for their views or choices
  2: Follow up others' points and show whether they agree or disagree in whole-class discussion
  9: Use beginning, middle and end to write narratives in which events are sequenced logically and conflicts resolved
  9: Write non-narrative texts using structures of different text-types

- **Cross-curricular links**
  Citizenship: animals and us

- **Assessing Pupils' Progress**
  Reading: AF1, AF2, AF3
  Writing: AF1, AF2, AF3, AF6
  Speaking and listening: AF1, AF2, AF3

CPL Pupil Book 3 Unit 1

Introduction

Overview

This is an amusing narrative in which a group of friends discover a very sad dragon.

Before you read

- **SL: AF2**

Ask if the children believe in dragons. Discuss how such mythical creatures might have come about. Stories are passed down through generations by word-of-mouth and so distortions, embellishments and so on are inevitable.

Tell the children the story of St George and the Dragon.

Answers

Do you remember?

Word selection

- **R: AF1, AF2**

Copy these sentences. Choose the correct word to fill each gap.

1. Mimi found a *dragon*.

2. The dragon was very *long*.

3. His name was *Duncan*.

4. He seemed rather *sad*.

5. Duncan had lost his *fire*.

More to think about

| Literal and deductive answering in sentences |

- R: AF2, AF3; W: AF6

Write a sentence to answer each question.

1. How many friends were on the beach?
   There were four friends on the beach.

2. Do you think they went to the beach to look for dragons?
   No, they didn't go to the beach to look for dragons.

3. Why were they going to run away?
   They were going to run away because they were frightened of the dragon.

4. Why had Duncan lost his fire?
   Duncan's cold had put out his fire.

5. Why did Duncan's family send him away?
   They sent him away because they said no one wants a dragon without fire.

Now try these

| Prediction; lists – assessing and evaluating; character empathy |

- R: AF3; W: AF1

1. What do you think happened next in the story? Write your own ending.
   (Children's own answer.)

   Notes: *This question calls for pupils to think back over the story in order to predict the outcome.*

2. Make two lists in your book.

   List 1: The best things about being a dragon.
   For example: breath fire, big, scary, can fly.

   List 2: The worst things about being a dragon.
   For example: no other dragons to play with, people scared of you, people think you are fierce.

3. Write about how you would have felt if you were Duncan and your family sent you away.
   (Children's own answer.)

   Notes: *These activities are intended to encourage empathy with the main character. Question 2 is also an early stage of assembling an argument.*

Enrichment

- Ask if any of the children have ever found anything strange or interesting on a beach. Talk about beachcombing and why people do it. (SL: AF1)

- Discuss how the children feel about the dragon in the story. Ask what they would have done had they been the children on the beach. (R: AF3; SL: AF2)

- Ask the children to imagine that they were one of the children on the beach. Ask them to write a first-person report of the event from the child's point of view. (R: AF3; W: AF2)

- The children can turn this extract into a short play to perform to the rest of the class. Ask them to write the playscript in groups before assigning roles and practising their performance. (SL: AF3)

 Resource Sheet 10A (R: AF2; W: AF6)

 Resource Sheet 10B
(R: AF2; W: AF2, AF3)

Further reading

The Kingfisher Treasury of Dragon Stories by Margaret Clark and Mark Robertson (Kingfisher, 2005);
The Little Dragon by Heather Amery and Stephen Cartwright (Usborne, 2003);
The Tale of Custard the Dragon by Ogden Nash and Lynn Munsinger (Little, Brown 1998).

The Dragon's Cold

Name _____ **Date** _____

Write a sentence to answer each question.

1. Who found a dragon?

_____

2. Was the dragon long or short?

_____

3. What was the dragon's name?

_____

4. Was the dragon happy?

_____

_____

5. What had the dragon lost?

_____

_____

6. Why wasn't the dragon with his friends?

_____

_____

The Dragon's Cold

Name _____   **Date** _____

You are the reporter for *The Sandy Beach News*, the local newspaper.
You were sent to investigate the amazing story of the children who found
a dragon on the beach!
Write an exciting and interesting report.
Don't forget to start with a good, strong headline.

Headline box

```



```

From our special reporter _____

_____

_____

_____

_____

_____

_____

Crash!

Narrative: adventure and mystery

Planning

- **Learning objectives**
  - 7: Infer characters' feelings in fiction and consequences in logical explanations
  - 8: Empathise with characters and debate moral dilemmas portrayed in texts
  - 9: Use beginning, middle and end to write narratives in which events are sequenced logically and conflicts resolved
  - 9: Use layout, format graphics and illustrations for different purposes

- **Cross-curricular links**
  Citizenship: people who help us

- **Assessing Pupils' Progress**
  Reading: AF1, AF2, AF3
  Writing: AF3, AF6, AF7

CPL Pupil Book 3 Unit 10

Introduction

Overview

This progress unit can be used to check progress in a more formal setting. No additional activities or preparation are suggested, but the questions in the *Pupil Book* should be familiar to children if they have worked through previous units. The questions require children to apply literal, deductive, evaluative and inferential comprehension skills to the words and pictures in this unit.

Before you read

Before undertaking the assessment read through the passage with the children to ensure all can read the extract because it is comprehension of the passage, not reading ability, which is being assessed.

Answers

Do you remember?

- R: AF1, AF2
- Award one mark for each correct answer (maximum six marks).

Copy these sentences. Choose words from the picture story to fill each gap.

1. The girls were looking out of their *window*.

2. They saw an aeroplane *crash* into the sea.

3. The pilot came down with his *parachute*.

4. The girls called for *help*.

5. A *helicopter* went to rescue the pilot.

6. The pilot gave the girls a *reward* for saving his life.

More to think about

Writing sentences; interpreting pictures; character empathy

- R: AF3; W: AF6
- Q1 award up to two marks for each sentence, depending on content and punctuation. Q2 award up to two marks for each answer, depending on the extent to which the child is empathising with the characters, as well as taking account of the content and punctuation (maximum 18 marks).

1. Write a sentence to explain what is happening in each of the six pictures.
   (Children's own answer.)

2. Look at the pictures and think about what the characters are saying. Write:
   a) three questions the telephone operator asked when the girls called.
   b) what the pilot said when the helicopter arrived.
   c) what the pilot said when he gave the girls a reward.
   (Children's own answer.)

Notes: *These questions call for pupils to empathise with each character.*

Now try these

Sequencing

- W: AF2, AF3, AF7
- Award up to six marks, depending on the extent to which the child is providing a logical sequence and is adding relevant words (maximum six marks).

Draw your own picture story for one of these events. Then add two words to describe each picture in your story.

1. an escape

2. an earthquake

3. a discovery

(Children's own answer.)

Indicative scores for National Curriculum

Below level 2	Level 2	Level 3
0–9	10–23	24–30

Indicative scores for Curriculum for Excellence

Early	First	Second
0–11	12–25	24–30

Non-fiction: information texts

Planning

- **Learning objectives**
  - 7: Identify how different texts are organised, including reference texts, magazines and leaflets, on paper and on screen
  - 1: Sustain conversation, explain or give reasons for their views or choices
  - 2: Follow up others' points and show whether they agree or disagree in whole-class discussion
  - 3: Actively include and respond to all members of the group
  - 9: Write non-narrative texts using structures of different text-types
  - 9: Use layout, format graphics and illustrations for different purposes

- **Cross-curricular links**
  PE: outdoor and adventurous activities

- **Assessing Pupils' Progress**
  Reading: AF1, AF2, AF3, AF4, AF6
  Writing: AF2, AF3, AF6
  Speaking and listening: AF2

CPL Pupil Book 3 Unit 11

Introduction

Overview

This is a poster for a young persons' biking event. The unit focuses on providing information for the specific purposes of attracting attention and getting information across.

Before you read

- **SL: AF2; R: AF4, AF6**

Ask the children to look at the poster and discuss whether or not they find it attractive and eye-catching. Ask if it would make them want to enter the event.

Talk about who the poster is aimed at. Ask the children if there is anything they would change about the poster to make it more appealing to the target audience.

Answers

Do you remember?

Selecting sentence endings

- **R: AF1, AF2**

Copy these sentences. Choose the correct ending to finish each sentence.

1. There is going to be a *bike-riding championship*.
2. It will be held on *Saturday 25th October*.
3. Junior events are *in the morning*.
4. Riders under 7 *are not allowed to ride*.
5. The entrance fee for spectators *is £1*.

More to think about

- R: AF2, AF3; W: AF6

1. Write a sentence to answer each question.
   a) Where are the championships to be held?
      *The championships are being held at
      Crossfield Farm (and/or Westergate).*
   b) How much does it cost to enter?
      *There is no charge for riders, but
      spectators must pay £1.*
   c) If you are 9, what time are your races?
      *Races for 9 year olds are between 10.00
      and 12.30.*
   d) Your sister is 13. What time are her races?
      *My sister's races would be between 12.30
      and 3.00.*
   e) Can you buy food and drinks after the
      races?
      Yes, food and drinks can be bought.

2. Copy these lists of words. Draw lines to join
   the words that have similar meanings. One
   has been done to help you.
   annual → once a year
   championship → competition
   fee → charge
   spectators → audience
   refreshments → things to eat and drink

Now try these

- R: AF3; W: AF2, AF3

1. Write some sentences to describe how you
   would feel if each of these things happened.
   a) You are given a new mountain bike as a
      present.
   b) The car taking you to the championships
      breaks down on the way.
   c) You win your first ever race.
   d) You reach the final, but then come last!
   e) Your little sister wins the cup in her event.
   (Children's own answer.)

   Notes: *Children will need to use empathy
   to 'think themselves into' each of these
   situations and explore their feelings. It will be
   helpful, although not essential, to discuss
   some, if not all, of these questions before
   children write the answers. Encourage the
   written answers to be presented in sentences,
   with correct punctuation.*

2. Design a poster for a running race. Think
   carefully about what you would need to know
   if you wanted to enter.

   Notes: *Ensure children are encouraged to
   plan carefully before embarking on this task.
   First make notes about what should be
   included on the poster and also prepare a
   small pencil sketch before drawing it.*

Enrichment

- Encourage the children to share their
  thoughts, ideas and aspirations about having
  a bike. (SL: AF2)

- The children can discuss, in groups, the
  issues of road safety and share experiences
  of when and why they should be extremely
  careful when riding in public areas – both for
  themselves and for other people around them.
  (SL: AF2)

- Ask the children, in pairs, to make a poster,
  similar to the one for the championship,
  encouraging the safe use of bikes. Remind
  the children that the poster should be striking
  and eye-catching, as well as giving all the
  necessary information. (W: AF2, AF3)

 Resource Sheet 11A (R: AF2; W: AF6)

 Resource Sheet 11B (W: AF2, AF3)

Further reading

Cycling (Training to Succeed) by Rita Storey (Franklin Watts, 2010);
Cycling (Sports Science) by James Bow (Franklin Watts, 2009).

Website: www.thinkroadsafety.gov.uk/arrivealive

Name _____   **Date** _____

Spot the mistake in each sentence.
Write each sentence with the correct information.

1. There is going to be a road safety competition.

_____

2. It will be held on Friday 25th October.

_____

3. Junior events are in the afternoon.

_____

4. Riders under 11 are not allowed to take part.

_____

5. There is no entrance fee for spectators.

_____

Fun on Bikes

Name _____   **Date** _____

You have been asked to design the track for
the Young Bikers' Championship.

It is important that you put detailed captions and notes on your plan
so that everyone building it knows what is needed.

The Owl Who Was Afraid of the Dark

Narrative: stories with familiar settings; significant authors

Planning

- **Learning objectives**
  7: Infer characters' feelings in fiction and consequences in logical explanations
  8: Empathise with characters and debate moral dilemmas portrayed in texts
  1: Sustain conversation, explain or give reasons for their views or choices
  2: Follow up others' points and show whether they agree or disagree in whole-class discussion
  3: Actively include and respond to all members of the group
  9: Use beginning, middle and end to write narratives in which events are sequenced logically and conflicts resolved

- **Cross-curricular links**
  Science: plants and animals in the local environment; habitats
  Citizenship: living in a diverse world

- **Assessing Pupils' Progress**
  Reading: AF1, AF2, AF3, AF5
  Writing: AF1, AF7
  Speaking and listening: AF1, AF2, AF4

CPL Pupil Book 3 Unit 1

Introduction

Overview

Plop is a baby owl. He is perfect in every way – except for one. He's afraid of the dark! But he soon discovers, through a variety of new friends, that the dark can be fun, exciting and magical. In this extract he meets a young girl.

Before you read

- SL: AF1, AF2

Talk about owls and their nocturnal habit. Ask the children to suggest other creatures which are active at night and sleep during daylight hours.

Ask the children to volunteer reasons why Plop might be afraid of the dark.

Author biography

- **Jill Tomlinson** trained as an opera singer but due to illness had to change careers.

- She started on a journalism course, but soon realised that she wanted to write for children.

- Her first story, 'The Bus who went to Church', was rejected by 16 publishers before it was accepted and she became one of our leading children's authors.

Answers

Do you remember?

Selecting correct answers

- R: AF1, AF2

Match these questions and answers. Write the answers in the correct order.

1. Where was the little girl?
   The little girl was below the tree.

2. Why did Plop think the girl had a tail?
   The girl's hair was in a pony-tail.

3. Could Plop fly well?
   No, Plop couldn't fly very well.

4. What sort of owl was Plop?
   Plop was a Barn Owl.

More to think about

- **R: AF2, AF3, AF5**

1. Which words in the story tell us that:
   a) Plop was worried about flying?
      Plop shut his eyes, took a deep breath
   b) he didn't yet have his adult feathers?
      woolly ball/fluffy tummy
   c) the little girl had dirty hands?
      grubby

2. Write three sentences in your book about Plop. Think about his personality as well as what he looks like.
   (Children's own answer.)

   Notes: *Answers may refer to Plop's age; fear of flying; bravery and determination; his roundness and fluffy appearance.*

3. Why do you think some of the words in the story are in darker print?

   Notes: *The bold type is a method of providing emphasis to some key words. Use the opportunity, as appropriate, to introduce the term 'bold type'.*

Now try these

Interpreting language; summarising

- **W: AF1, AF7**

1. The little girl said Plop was like a 'woolly ball'. Write some words to describe these birds and animals.
   a) giraffe: *tall, graceful, slender, thin, agile*
   b) hippopotamus: *huge, lumbering, patient, aggressive*
   c) robin: *delicate, friendly, chirpy*
   d) kitten: *inquisitive, cuddly, fluffy, playful*

   Note: *answers may also refer to their colours.*

2. Have you ever been frightened of the dark, like Plop? Make a list of the things about the dark that can sometimes frighten people.
   (Children's own answer.)

   Notes: *This is an opportunity for children to explore the common fear of the dark. Useful discussions can enable the children to share their feelings, but also to discover that most such fears are groundless. Collate the anxieties into a list and incorporate into a wall display.*

Enrichment

- Many children are afraid of the dark, so this is a good opportunity to discuss the anxieties that might be shared by the children. (SL: AF2)

- In groups, the children can read aloud some poems about night and darkness and talk about how the poets describe these things. (R: AF5; SL: AF4)

- Discuss how important darkness is (providing a period in which most people and animals sleep, which refreshes and 'recharges' their bodies) and what causes it (the Earth spinning and showing a different area to the Sun). (SL: AF2)

- Ask the children to write a short story with a similar theme, where a young creature is afraid of something. For example, the frog who is afraid of water, the eagle who is afraid of heights. (W: AF1)

 Resource Sheet 12A (R: AF2)

 Resource Sheet 12B (W: AF1)

Further reading

Also by Jill Tomlinson: *The Penguin Who Wanted to Find Out* (Egmont Books, 2004);
The Aardvark Who Wasn't Sure (Egmont Books, 2004);
The Cat Who Wanted to Go Home (Egmont Books, 2006);
The Otter Who Wanted to Know (Egmont Books, 2004).

The Owl Who Was Afraid of the Dark

Name _____ **Date** _____

Choose a word from the box to fill each gap.

| bounced | girl | Barn | pony-tail | Tawny | ball | tail |

1. Mother Owl told Plop to talk to the little _____.

2. The girl had her hair in a _____.

3. She thought Plop was a woolly _____.

4. Plop said he was a _____ Owl.

5. She thought he was a ball because he _____.

6. He told her _____ Owls say 'Tu-wit-a-woo'.

7. Plop told her she wasn't a proper girl because

   she had a _____.

Unit 12B

The Owl Who Was Afraid of the Dark

Name _____ **Date** _____

Imagine you meet a young frog who can talk.
He is sitting on the side of a pond, but he is afraid of the water.
Finish writing the conversation.

Me   Hi there, Frog. Why are you looking so sad?

Frog   I'm not sad. But I am a bit scared. I don't think I like water.

Me   Why don't you like water? You're a frog!

_____

_____

_____

_____

_____

_____

_____

Non-fiction: instructions

Planning

- **Learning objectives**
  7: Identify how different texts are organised, including reference texts, magazines and leaflets, on paper and on screen
  1: Sustain conversation, explain or give reasons for their views or choices
  2: Follow up others' points and show whether they agree or disagree in whole-class discussion
  9: Write non-narrative texts using structures of different text-types
  9: Use layout, format graphics and illustrations for different purposes

- **Cross-curricular links**
  Science: habitats
  Geography: geography and numbers

- **Assessing Pupils' Progress**
  Reading: AF1, AF2, AF3, AF4
  Writing: AF2, AF3, AF6
  Speaking and listening: AF1, AF2

CPL Pupil Book 3 Unit 6

Introduction

Overview

This is a map of the zoo that Dinesh and Indira are visiting with their grandparents. The unit is about interpreting and creating instructional texts, diagrams and maps.

Before you read

- SL: AF2; R: AF4

Show and talk about some maps – use world atlases, road atlases and wall maps. Discuss their different functions and value. Allow the children to study the maps in groups.

Answers

Do you remember?

Cloze from passage

- R: AF1, AF2

Copy these sentences. Fill each gap.

1. The children's names are *Dinesh* and *Indira*.

2. Their *grandparents* had taken them to the zoo.

3. They were feeding the *lambs*.

4. They didn't notice they were *lost*.

5. Luckily Indira had a *map of the zoo*.

More to think about

Interpreting map

- R: AF2, AF3; W: AF6

Write a sentence to answer each question. Use the map to find the answers.

1. Where were Dinesh and Indira feeding the lambs?
   They were feeding the lambs in Pets' Corner.

2. Describe their quickest way back to the ticket office?
   The quickest way to the ticket office was past the pelicans, flamingos, sea lions and lions.

3. Which animals are kept closest to the ticket office?
Lions are kept closest to the ticket office.

4. What type of sea animal would they have seen as they walked back to the office?
They would have seen a sea lion.

5. Grandad left a message at the office to meet at the exit. Describe the best route from the office to the exit.
Turn left at the monkey's enclosure.

6. Which creatures did they see sharing an enclosure with the pelicans?
Flamingoes were sharing an enclosure with the pelicans.

7. What animals were sharing with the zebras?
Deer were sharing with the zebras.

8. If they had gone to the exit straight from Pets' Corner, which two roads would they have walked along?
To reach the exit they would have walked along Bird Way and Bear Road.

Now try these

Character empathy; conveying information

- **W: AF2, AF3**

1. Can you remember ever being lost? Imagine you are Dinesh or Indira and you are lost in this crowded zoo on a very hot day. Write some sentences about how you are feeling and what you are thinking.
(Children's own answer.)

Notes: *Children will need to use empathy to 'think themselves into' this situation and explore their feelings. If possible, discuss this in groups first, encouraging the children to reflect on similar situations they may have experienced.*

2. There is a visitor coming to your classroom. Write clear instructions that tell the visitor how to get from the school entrance to your classroom.
(Children's own answer.)

Notes: *It might be helpful for the children to walk the route, taking notes, before undertaking this task. Alternatively, walk the route after the task to check its accuracy.*

Enrichment

- In groups, the children can share experiences of zoos and animal parks that they have visited. If possible ask the children to find the places mentioned on a map, probably a road atlas. Ask the children to try to interpret the map to describe how they reached the zoo from their home. (R: AF2; SL: AF2)

- Discuss what it feels like to be lost. If any of the children have been lost, ask how they felt and what happened. (SL: AF1)

- Discuss what actions the children should take if they become lost to ensure they stay safe. They might, for example, approach adults

who have children of their own, or go to someone in uniform (police, security officer, first-aider). Ask the children, in pairs, to design a poster or write a set of rules to follow when lost. (SL: AF2; W: AF2)

- Ask the children to either draw a simple map or write directions to describe how they travel between home and school, or between two other well-known places. (W: AF2)

 Resource Sheet 13A (R: AF2)

 Resource Sheet 13B (W: AF2)

Further reading

Collins Primary World Atlas (Collins, 2010).

Unit 13A

Lost in the Zoo

Name _____ **Date** _____

Choose a word from the box to fill each gap.

| Dinesh | map | lambs | lost | Indira | pelicans |
| Church Street | | elephant | grandparents | | |

1. _____ and _____ have been taken to the zoo.

2. Their _____ took them there.

3. They fed the _____ in Pets' Corner.

4. They didn't notice they were _____.

5. Indira had a _____ of the zoo in her pocket.

6. Their grandparents were looking at the flamingos and _____ by the pool.

7. They stopped to see the _____ near the exit.

8. They walked along _____ _____ on the way home.

Lost in the Zoo

Unit 13B

On the map, draw a line showing how you would walk from Pet's Corner to the church.

Describe this route to a friend who doesn't have a map.

The Tale of Peter Rabbit

Narrative: stories with familiar settings; significant authors

Planning

- **Learning objectives**
  7: Infer characters' feelings in fiction and consequences in logical explanations
  8: Share and compare reasons for reading preferences, extending the range of books read
  8: Empathise with characters and debate moral dilemmas portrayed in texts
  1: Sustain conversation, explain or give reasons for their views or choices
  2: Follow up others' points and show whether they agree or disagree in whole-class discussion
  4: Present events and characters through dialogue to engage the interest of an audience
  9: Use beginning, middle and end to write narratives in which events are sequenced logically and conflicts resolved

- **Cross-curricular links**
  Science: plants and animals in the local environment

- **Assessing Pupils' Progress**
  Reading: AF1, AF2, AF3
  Writing: AF1, AF6
  Speaking and listening: AF1, AF2, AF3

CPL Pupil Book 3 Unit 1

Introduction

Overview

This is an extract from the Beatrix Potter classic *The Tale of Peter Rabbit*. Peter ventures into Mr McGregor's garden to help himself to some vegetables.

Before you read

- SL: AF1, AF2

Ask the children if any of their parents or grandparents grow vegetables. Discuss why some people grow vegetables when they can be readily purchased in the shops.

Ask if any of the children already know *The Tale of Peter Rabbit* and what they think about it.

Author biography

- **Helen Beatrix Potter** was born in 1866 and died in 1943.

- She is famous for the anthropomorphic characters in her children's books.

- She is also widely respected for her knowledge of fungi.

- She wanted to marry Norman Warne, her publisher, but the marriage was blocked by her parents and he died before they could marry.

- With her royalties she bought farms in the Lake District in North West England, most of which have been left to the nation.

- She wrote and illustrated 23 books.

Answers

Do you remember?

Finishing sentences

- **R: AF1, AF2**

Copy these sentences. Fill each gap.

1. Mrs Rabbit told her children they must not *go into Mr McGregor's garden*.

2. Flopsy, Mopsy and Cotton-tail went to gather *blackberries*.

3. Peter got into Mr McGregor's garden by *squeezing under the gate*.

4. When Mr McGregor saw Peter he *jumped up and ran after him*.

More to think about

Deductive answering in sentences; vocabulary work

- **R: AF2, AF3; W: AF6**

1. Write a sentence to answer each question.
   a) What had happened to Mr Rabbit?
      Mr Rabbit had been put into a pie.
   b) What did Peter eat in the garden?
      Peter ate some lettuce, French beans and radishes.
   c) What was Mr McGregor doing in the garden?
      Mr McGregor was planting out young cabbages.
   d) Why did Mr McGregor call Peter a "thief"?
      He called Peter a thief because he had taken the food without asking.

2. Copy these words from the story. Then next to each, write another word the writer could have used. One has been done to help you.
   a) mischief: *trouble/problems/scrapes*
   b) naughty: *badly behaved/disobedient*
   c) gather: *collect/pick*
   d) squeezed: *slid/squashed*

Now try these

Incident empathy; prediction

- **R: AF3; W: AF1**

1. In your book write what Mr McGregor might have said to his wife when he went in for his tea.
   (Children's own answer.)

   Notes: *Encourage children to think carefully about clues to Mr McGregor's personality, and the history of the situation.*

2. Do you think Peter escaped from the garden? Write your own ending to this story.
   (Children's own answer.)

Enrichment

- Ask how the children would react if they found a rabbit eating their food. Discuss how humans and animals co-exist. (SL: AF2)

- Ask the children to share their answers to 'Now try these', question 2, by reading them aloud to the class. Allow the children to discuss and comment on the proposed endings. (SL: AF1)

- Ask the children, in pairs, to act out the story, taking it in turns to play each part. (SL: AF3)

 Resource Sheet 14A (R: AF2; W: AF6)

 Resource Sheet 14B (W: AF1)

Further reading

Also by Beatrix Potter: *The Tale of Squirrel Nutkin* (Frederick Warne, 2002);
The Tale of Little Pig Robinson (Frederick Warne, 2002);
The Tale of Mrs Tittlemouse (Frederick Warne, 2002).

The Tale of Peter Rabbit

Unit 14A

Name _____   **Date** _____

Spot the mistake in each sentence.
Write each sentence correctly.

1. Mrs Rabbit told her children they must run along and get into mischief.

_____

2. Flopsy, Mopsy and Peter went to gather blackberries.

_____

3. Peter squeezed under Mr McGregor's fence.

_____

4. When Mr McGregor saw Peter he waved his spade.

_____

5. Peter called Mr McGregor a "thief".

_____

Unit 14B

The Tale of Peter Rabbit

Name _____   **Date** _____

1. Write in the speech bubbles what you think Peter Rabbit's mother says to him when he gets home and what Peter replies.

_____
_____
_____

Peter's mother

_____
_____
_____

Peter

2. Now draw and write the speech bubbles to show what happens next.

On Holiday

Non-fiction: instructions

Planning

- **Learning objectives**

  7: Identify how different texts are organised, including reference texts, magazines and leaflets, on paper and on screen

  1: Sustain conversation, explain or give reasons for their views or choices

  2: Follow up others' points and show whether they agree or disagree in whole-class discussion

  9: Write non-narrative texts using structures of different text-types

- **Cross-curricular links**

  Geography: geography and numbers; going to the seaside

  Citizenship: how do rules and laws affect me?

- **Assessing Pupils' Progress**

  Reading: AF1, AF2, AF3, AF4

  Writing: AF2, AF6

  Speaking and listening: AF1, AF2

CPL Pupil Book 3 Unit 6

Vocabulary

provisions – supplies of food and household items
unaccompanied – without supervision

Introduction

Overview

A family has just arrived at a holiday park. They find an instruction leaflet and a simple map waiting for them.

Before you read

- **SL: AF1, AF2; R: AF4**

Ask the children to share experiences of any sort of holiday or day trips they've been on. Ask if they remember any rules or instructions from their holiday or day trip.

Look at the map with the children and explain how distances can be measured using the scale. Make sure the children understand all the symbols used on the map.

Answers

Do you remember?

Cloze from passage

- **R: AF1, AF2**

Copy these sentences. Fill each gap.

1. Jo's family went to *Sandy Bay Holiday Park* for their holiday.

2. When they arrived they were given *three* instructions and five *rules*.

3. *Leaflets* were available in the information centre.

4. Nobody was allowed in the swimming pool after *6 pm*.

More to think about

- R: AF3, AF4; W: AF6

1. Write a sentence to answer each question. You might need to use a ruler.
   a) How far is it to the beach?
      It's about half a mile (one kilometre) to the beach.
   b) What is the nearest town?
      The nearest town is Moreton.
   c) How far is it to the Motor Sports theme park?
      It is one mile to the Motor Sports theme park.
   d) What might be the best thing for the family to do when it rains?
      The family could go to the indoor amusement park when it rains.

2. What does each of these phrases mean?
   a) help you find your feet
      help you settle in quickly
   b) to stock up with provisions
      to buy food and other essential requirements
   c) get your bearings
      learn where everything is
   d) away from the hurly-burly of everyday life
      away from work and problems of normal living.

Now try these

- R: AF3; W: AF2

Notes: *These activities require consideration of the reasons for, and desirability and acceptability of, certain situations. Such work is often enhanced if preceded by oral work in a group or class lesson.*

1. Explain why the holiday park thinks each rule will make the holiday more relaxed for all the guests.
   (Children's own answer.)

2. Pretend you are Jo. Write a postcard to a friend telling him or her what you are doing on holiday.
   (Children's own answer.)

Enrichment

- Discuss with the children why rules and laws are needed when groups of people are living, working or playing together. Do they think the rules for Sandy Bay are reasonable? Are there others they would suggest? Talk about the difference between 'rules' and 'advice'. (SL: AF2)

- Distribute maps among the children and give each group specific tasks to practise interpreting the symbols and measuring distances. (R: AF2, AF4)

- Ask the children to write a set of rules and offer advice and suggestions that might be given to new children when they first arrive at your school. Resource Sheet 15B can be used as a template. (W: AF2)

 Resource Sheet 15A (R: AF2)

 Resource Sheet 15B (W: AF2)

Further reading

Collins Primary World Atlas (Collins, 2010);
Where on Earth? by Scoular Anderson (Collins Big Cat, 2005).

Hot Dog Harris

Name _____   **Date** _____

Using books or the internet, find the record for the smallest dog living now.

1. Make notes about the size of the dog and where it lives.

_____

_____

_____

2. Now research the biggest dog in the world and make notes.

_____

_____

_____

3. Imagine you owned this dog.
   Describe what it is like when you take him for a walk.

_____

_____

_____

_____

Funny Feeders

Planning

- **Learning objectives**
  7: Identify how different texts are organised, including reference texts, magazines and leaflets, on paper and on screen
  7: Identify and make notes of the main points of section(s) of text
  1: Sustain conversation, explain or give reasons for their views or choices
  2: Follow up others' points and show whether they agree or disagree in whole-class discussion
  9: Write non-narrative texts using structures of different text-types

- **Cross-curricular links**
  Science: teeth and eating; variation

- **Assessing Pupils' Progress**
  Reading: AF1, AF2, AF3, AF4
  Writing: AF1, AF6
  Speaking and listening: AF1, AF2

CPL Pupil Book 3 Unit 11

Vocabulary

parasite – an animal or plant that lives in or on another (the host) from which it obtains nourishment

Introduction

Overview

This is an information text with sub-headings and photographic illustration, giving information about the unusual feeding habits of some animals.

Before you read

- **SL: AF2; R: AF4**

Discuss the use of reference books to gather information. Talk about indexes and contents pages and how they might appear in relation to this passage.

Share and discuss the notion that all living things need food and water to sustain life. Discuss what happens when one or both of these is unavailable for a period of time, for example, the effect of drought on humans, animals and plant life.

Answers

Do you remember?

Cloze from passage

- R: AF1, AF2

Copy these sentences. Fill each gap.

1. Some frogs have long *tongues*.

2. Vultures wait for animals to *die* (or *be killed*).

3. Venus fly traps catch *insects* in their leaves.

4. Mistletoe grows in *(the branches of) trees*.

5. Mosquitoes and fleas are both called *parasites*.

More to think about

Deductive answering in sentences

- R: AF3; W: AF6

Write a sentence to answer each question.

1. Why are vultures good for the environment?
   They clear away dead creatures which could spread diseases.

2. Why would it be bad for the parasite if it killed the plant or animal it lives on?
   If a parasite kills its 'host' it destroys its home and supply of food.

3. Why do you think mistletoe becoming a rare plant in many places?
   Answers may include: over-harvesting for Christmas; fewer birds to transport seeds; fewer trees (especially following Dutch Elm Disease).

4. If you squash a mosquito it leaves a red mark. Why?
   The red is blood from previous feeds.

Now try these

Character empathy; imaginative description

- R: AF3; W: AF1

1. Imagine that you are a creature that has just arrived from outer space. You have never seen humans before. Write a report about how these strange human creatures feed.
   (Children's own answer.)

   Notes: *This activity is devised to encourage detailed, close analysis of a common function of human behaviour. Other functions, such as walking, sleeping, or games, could have the same activity applied to them.*

2. Imagine that you are either a frog or a vulture. Write about how you feel as you watch and wait for your food.
   (Children's own answer.)

Enrichment

- Discuss the idea of a food chain. Ask the children, in groups, to research carnivorous, herbivorous and omnivorous creatures, then make lists of creatures that fall into each group. Use Resource Sheet 19B as a template. (R: AF2)

- Provide reference books for the children to explore in pairs. Ask them to find specific information using the index, then make notes about a certain topic. (R: AF2)

- Recap the purpose of different features of a reference book. Ask individual children to explain certain features. (R: AF4; SL: AF1)

 Resource Sheet 19A (R: AF2)

 Resource Sheet 19B (R: AF2)

Further reading

Fabulous Creatures: Are They Real? by Scoular Anderson (Collins Big Cat, 2005);
Think Again! by Geraldine McCaughrean (Collins Big Cat, 2005);
Weird Little Monsters by Nic Bishop (Collins Big Cat, 2007).

Funny Feeders

Name _____   **Date** _____

Choose a word from the box to fill each gap.

> plants   trees   tongues   parasites   die   blood   insects

1. Some frogs have long _____.

2. Vultures wait for animals to _____.

3. Venus fly traps catch _____ in their leaves.

4. Some plants can live off other _____.

5. Mistletoe grows in _____.

6. Mosquitoes and fleas are both called _____.

7. Mosquitoes and fleas both suck _____ from other creatures.

Unit 19B Funny Feeders

Name _____ **Date** _____

Use books or the internet to research the answers to these questions and fill in the table.

1. What is a carnivorous creature?

   _____

2. What is a herbivorous creature?

   _____

3. What is an omnivorous creature?

   _____

4. Fill in the table with names of animals.

Carnivorous creatures	Herbivorous creatures	Omnivorous creatures

5. What are you? _____

Mrs Wobble the Waitress

Narrative: stories with familiar settings; significant authors

Planning

- **Learning objectives**
  - 7: Infer characters' feelings in fiction and consequences in logical explanations
  - 7: Identify and make notes of the main points of section(s) of text
  - 8: Empathise with characters and debate moral dilemmas portrayed in texts
  - 1: Sustain conversation, explain or give reasons for their views or choices
  - 2: Follow up others' points and show whether they agree or disagree in whole-class discussion
  - 3: Actively include and respond to all members of the group
  - 9: Use beginning, middle and end to write narratives in which events are sequenced logically and conflicts resolved
  - 9: Write non-narrative texts using structures of different text-types

- **Cross-curricular links**
  Citizenship: living in a diverse world

- **Assessing Pupils' Progress**
  Reading: AF1, AF2, AF3
  Writing: AF1, AF2, AF6
  Speaking and listening: AF1, AF2

CPL Pupil Book 3 Unit 1

Introduction

Overview

This is an amusing narrative extract about Mrs Wobble the Waitress (from the series *Happy Families*) who finds it difficult to carry food out to her customers.

Before you read

- SL: AF1, AF2

Discuss the attributes that are needed for a job waitressing in a café or restaurant.

Ask the children which jobs they would like to do and discuss what skills might be required for those jobs.

Author biography

- **Allan Ahlberg** was born near London in 1938.

- He was a teacher for ten years before he wrote his first book, *The Brick Street Boys*.

- Allan collaborated with his wife Janet, who illustrated many of his prize-winning titles, before she sadly died in 1994.

- They worked closely together in a process he described as 'getting an idea and batting it around, like table tennis'.

- Allan has continued to write collections and picture books as well as novels and poetry, most of which are inspired by his years as a teacher.

Answers

Do you remember?

Reversing sentences

- R: AF1, AF2

Here are the answers to four questions about the story. Write the question for each one. One has been done to help you.

1. Mrs Wobble keeps dropping the food she is serving.
   What does Mrs Wobble keep dropping?

2. She is very worried.
   How does Mrs Wobble feel about serving food?

3. The Wobble children catch the food.
   Who catches the food that Mrs Wobble drops?

4. The customers think it is fun.
   What do the customers think about the food being dropped and caught?

More to think about

Working with phrases; deductive
answering in sentences

- R: AF2, AF3; W: AF6

1. Choose words from each column to make sentences about the story.
   Their sentences should be:
   Mrs Wobble was very upset when she lost her job.
   Master Wobble skated to the rescue to catch the chicken.
   Miss Wobble skated to the rescue to catch the soup.

2. Write a sentence to answer each question.
   a) Why did the customers cheer?
      The customers cheered out of relief.
   b) Why did the customers think their meal was "more fun than a circus"?
      They thought that the activities and atmosphere in the restaurant was very entertaining.

Now try these

Summarising; outcome prediction;
critical evaluation of content

- R: AF3; W: AF1, AF2

1. Write a summary of the story of Mrs Wobble the Waitress in your own words. Your summary should be no more than 40 words.
   (Children's own answer.)

   Notes: *This summary writing can be difficult for some children. Support the children by having an initial discussion (class or groups) to isolate the main idea and key events.*

2. Write a few sentences to tell how you think the story might finish. Try to make it interesting or funny.
   (Children's own answer.)

   Notes: *This requires children to have understood the story in order to predict possible outcomes. Choose other, similar stories to be read aloud to the class.*

3. Write a set of rules to make sure your kitchen at home is a safe place.
   (Children's own answer.)

   Notes: *This question requires the children to draw on experience outside the text.*

Enrichment

- In groups, the children can discuss whether it was fair of Mrs Wobble's previous employer to sack her and, indeed, sensible for her family to set up a café for her in their own home. (R: AF3; SL: AF2)

- Talk about how both children and adults with disabilities can be enabled to participate as fully as possible in activities which they might otherwise find difficult. (SL: AF2)

- Ask the children to imagine they have a condition that means they can't stop shaking. Ask them to make a list of the things they might find most difficult to do. (W: AF2)

 Resource Sheet 20A (R: AF2; W: AF6)

 Resource Sheet 20B (W: AF2)

Further reading

Also by Allan and Janet Ahlberg:
Happy Family series:
Mrs Plug the Plumber (Puffin, 2005); *Mr Tick the Teacher* (Puffin, 2004); *Mr Biff the Boxer* (Puffin, 2005).
Funnybones series:
Funnybones (Puffin, 2010); *Dinosaur Dreams* (Puffin, 2005); *The Pet Shop* (Puffin, 2004);
Skeleton Crew (Puffin, 2005).

Mrs Wobble the Waitress

Name _____ **Date** _____

Write a sentence to answer each question.

1. What does Mrs Wobble keep dropping?

_____

2. Where did she used to work?

_____

3. Who has opened a café?

_____

4. What did the first customer order?

_____

5. Who caught the chicken?

_____

6. What did the customers say?

_____

Mrs Wobble the Waitress

Name _____   **Date** _____

The Wobble Family helped their mother when she had a problem.
Have you ever helped your parents or any other adult with a job?
Write a report about what needed to be done and how you helped.

The day I helped _____ to _____

_____

_____

_____

_____

_____

_____

_____

_____

_____

The Golly Sisters Go West

Narrative: dialogue and plays; significant authors

Planning

- **Learning objectives**
  7: Infer characters' feelings in fiction and consequences in logical explanations
  7: Identify and make notes of the main points of section(s) of text
  8: Empathise with characters and debate moral dilemmas portrayed in texts
  9: Use beginning, middle and end to write narratives in which events are sequenced logically and conflicts resolved

- **Cross-curricular links**
  Citizenship: animals and us
  Geography: where in the world is Barnaby Bear?

- **Assessing Pupils' Progress**
  Reading: AF1, AF2, AF3
  Writing: AF1, AF6

CPL Pupil Book 3 Unit 2

Vocabulary

west – in this context means the Wild West in America

Introduction

Overview

This progress unit can be used to check progress in a more formal setting. No additional activities or preparation are suggested, but the questions in the *Pupil Book* should be familiar to children if they have worked through previous units. The questions require children to apply literal, deductive, evaluative and inferential comprehension skills to the story in this unit.

Author biography

- **Betsy Byars** was born in 1928 in North Carolina, USA.

- She began her writing career by writing short magazine articles.

- She has written over 60 books for children, which have been translated into 19 languages.

- She now lives in South Carolina with her husband, Ed.

Before you read

Before undertaking the assessment read through the passage with the children to ensure all can read the extract because it is comprehension of the passage, not reading ability, which is being assessed.

Indicative scores for National Curriculum

Below level 2	Level 2	Level 3
0–9	10–25	26–30

Indicative scores for Curriculum for Excellence

Early	First	Second
0–11	12–26	27–30

Answers

Do you remember?

- R: AF1, AF2

- **Award one mark for each correct answer (maximum 11 marks).**

Copy this paragraph. Fill each gap.

May-May and *Rose*, the two Golly sisters, couldn't make their *horse* go. The *wagon* was loaded, and they had practised their *songs* and *dances*. The sisters got very *mad*, but the horse still wouldn't go! They walked around the *horse* but it still wouldn't *go*. Then Rose remembered you need to say *Giddy-up* to tell a horse to go. As soon as they said this the horse *went*.

More to think about

Correcting sentence content; deductive answering in sentences

- R: AF2, AF3; W: AF6

- **Q1 award one mark for each correct answer. Q2 award one mark for each correct answer (maximum 12 marks).**

1. One word in each of these sentences is not correct. Write each sentence correctly.
   a) May-May told the horse to *go*.
   b) May-May got down from the wagon *second*.
   c) Rose *could* tell that something was wrong.
   d) Rose remembered a *horse* word.

2. Write a sentence to answer each question.
   a) In which country do you think the Golly sisters lived?
      The Golly sisters lived in America.
   b) Where were the Golly sisters going?
      They were going west (across America).
   c) What work were they going to do when they got there?
      They were going to sing and dance.
   d) How do you know they didn't drive wagons very often?
      The sisters didn't know how to tell a horse to move forward.
   e) Was the horse well trained or badly trained?
      The horse was well trained.

f) Were they right to get cross with the horse?
   No, they were not right to get cross with the horse.
g) Did getting cross with the horse make it go?
   No, the horse didn't move when they got cross with it.
h) How did they make it go in the end?
   They used the horse word for go, giddy-up.

Now try these

Summary; inference; prediction; empathy

- R: AF3; W: AF1

- **Q1 award one mark for two components, two marks for three or more. Q2 maximum one mark for full answer: the horse will go when it gets the correct command, and it is difficult to control as it has a will of its own. Qs 3 and 4 maximum two marks available for each (maximum seven marks).**

1. Write a short version of the story so far, using no more than three sentences.
   (Children's own answer.)

   Notes: *The three most significant events for children to spot are: the sisters intending to go west (to earn their living as performers); their ignorance about driving a horse and wagon; the discovery that with the correct instruction the horse would move.*

2. What do you think the Golly sisters have learned from their experience with the horse?
   (Children's own answer.)

3. Write some sentences to tell how you think the story of the Golly sisters might have ended?
   (Children's own answer.)

   Notes: *Children may predict either short- or long-term outcomes.*

4. Imagine you really wanted to go somewhere, but for some reason you weren't able to get there. Write some sentences about what happened and how you felt.
   (Children's own answer.)

Notes